UP STREAM

AN AMERICAN CHRONICLE

UP STREAM

AN AMERICAN CHRONICLE

BY

LUDWIG LEWISOHN

BONI AND LIVERIGHT
PUBLISHERS : NEW YORK

UP STREAM

AN AMERICAN CHRONICLE

—

Copyright, 1922, by
BONI & LIVERIGHT, INC.

—

Printed in the United States of America
First Printing, March, 1922
Second Printing, May, 1922
Third Printing, June, 1922
Fourth Printing, June, 1922
Fifth Printing, July, 1922
Sixth Printing, August, 1922
Seventh Printing, September, 1922
Eighth Printing, November, 1922
Ninth Printing, December, 1922
Tenth Printing, April, 1923
Eleventh Printing, May, 1923
Twelfth Printing, July, 1923
Thirteenth Printing, December, 1923
Fourteenth Printing, February, 1924

THE PLIMPTON PRESS
NORWOOD · MASS · U·S·A

CONTENTS

PROLOGUE

The world is full of stories and many of the stories are true. But they are not true enough. An artistic pattern comes between the teller of the tale and his reality, or a vague fear of stupid and malicious comment or—especially in America—a desire to avoid singularity. Yet, somehow, we must master life or it will end by destroying us. We can master it only by understanding it and we can understand it only by telling each other the quite naked and, if need be, the devastating truth.

Some such perception and some such motive is in the consciousness of every serious novelist and in that of every thinker. But the novelist sacrifices to a form and the thinker to a system. Each has had an anterior vision into which he lets his facts and even his emotions melt. And this anterior vision—of a fable in the one case, of a logical structure in the other—is nothing but a mask. For both the novelist and the philosopher is only an autobiographer in disguise. Each writes a confession; each is a lyricist at bottom. I, too, could easily have written a novel or a treatise. I have chosen to drop the mask.

It is not a simple thing to do. One likes to be decorous. The folds of this mantle of civilization we wear in public, and often enough, in private, are graceful and accustomed. They give a dignity to the figure that the mind may lack. But if no one will ever speak out for fear of wounding his own susceptibilities or those of others, this hush of cowardly considerateness and moral stealth in which so much of our life is passed will either throttle us some day or sting us into raw and mad revolt.

In every other country men have spoken out in prose or verse and have recorded their experience and their vision and their judgment on this civilization in which we are ensnared. But no one has spoken out in America. We have not suffered enough, and man is a timid and a patient creature from whom nothing less than the unendurable itself will wring a protest. There are thousands of people among us who can find in my adventures a living symbol of theirs and in my conclusion a liberation of their own and in whom, as in me, this moment of history has burned away delusions to the last shred. But how many will admit that and not rather yield to the insidious fear of those to whom they owe deference or money or a social position in Gopher Prairie or Central City? It is a nice question which must be settled in each conscience. I have done my share.

CHAPTER I

A FAR CHILDHOOD

I

The city that I remember, the Berlin of the eighties, was rugged and grey. But it had nothing forbidding in its aspect, rather an air of homely and familiar comfort. There were few private houses, but people lived in their apartments in large, airy rooms with tall French windows and neat, white tile ovens. The streets were monotonous in appearance but admirably clean. There were no posters, no public advertisements except upon the pillars erected for that purpose, the traffic of horse-cars, omnibuses and cabs was orderly and convenient. The cabs, driven by red-faced, loquacious cabbies in blue-caped coats and top-hats, were cheap. My father and mother, though far from rich, used them constantly, and I remember being driven for hours through the black-draped city on that icy day in 1888 on which the old emperor's body lay in state in the cathedral.

My earliest glimpses of beauty are characteristic of the city. One was the windows of the Royal Porcelain Works on the Leipziger Strasse. With all the exquisite sensitiveness of childhood I saw those wonderful little figures and their porcelain veils and draperies and delicately moulded forms. They were so tiny and yet so perfect, and they thrilled me far more than Rauch's equestrian statue of the great Frederic or the chariot of victory over the city gate.

The latter were dutifully impressed upon me by my father; my mother let me stand and gaze my fill before the windows of the porcelain shop . . . But the great sight to me, which I never saw without a lifting of the heart, was a certain public square. One walked or drove through a short street in which villas stood in gardens; at the end of that street one came upon the square quite suddenly. To that moment I always looked forward; the sensation was like the sudden crash of an orchestra. For the square spread out with an airiness, a fine and noble amplitude of shape and proportion, a grace and majesty at once that I despair of rendering into words. I have seen nothing like it since. Perhaps it seemed finer to my childish eyes than it was or is; but I am willing to yield to that old vision as a true one, since the seat of beauty is after all in the beholding mind . . .

Beyond the square lay the Tiergarten. Thither I was taken on many pleasant afternoons. And I can still see very clearly the statue of Flora surrounded by gorgeous flower-beds and the monument to Queen Louise and the "snail hill" swarming with other children and their nurse-maids; I can still hear their merry cries; I can still feel the stinging coolness on my heated throat of the milk sold at the famous kiosks of Bolle. But when I was four or five years old I would beg my nurse to take me to the gold-fish pond. It was generally still by the little artificial lake and I loved the stillness; the dark green foilage was very thick all around and the dusk fell early there. The mute darting about of the fishes seemed mysterious and soothing, the stone benches were cool and strong and bare. I felt in this spot without knowing it, the majesty of places withdrawn from the cries of men ... Another scene of the great park I remember: a winter scene. Bare trees and the frozen river around the Rousseau Island and the gay scarfs of the skaters. And suddenly dusk and a brazen sun-disc black-barred by trees. Then the swift early winter night and the gas-lamps of the streets and the warmth and security of home ...

But the out-of-door scenes of winter that I recall are few: another square and the snow-flakes falling thick and my father and I walking across it to a Vienna café where he played chess on Sunday mornings. This is one scene. And another is our sturdy maid carrying me from a playmate's house to a cab through a blinding blizzard. And the third is the Christmas fair —long since abolished—on the Belle-Alliance Square. Twinkling lights in the frosty air, and booths noisy and gay with cheap toys and cakes, and everywhere the sharp odor of the fir-trees.

I loved spring more than even this—the cool, virginal, gradual spring of the North. The windows were opened and children reappeared on the streets and great boughs of lilacs were sold. Have the German lilacs a headier and sweeter fragrance than ours? It seemed to fill the air and the heart; it meant the winds of spring and people sitting in gardens and casting aside their cares. For the Germans, I can recognise now, yield to the natural moods of the seasons. Spring is to them still the spring of the folk-songs and they would like to pack a bundle and wander out into the land with lilac blossoms in their hats ... My father and mother took a cab on Sunday and drove in the Tiergarten or else went by boat up the river Spree to

Treptow and there we sat on pleasant terraces and watched the life on the water. Even then I loved to see men and youths in their skiffs with bare white arms and legs and paddles flashing in the sunlight and took a deep delight in the strong, silent, virile rhythm of the rise and fall of their oars. And my father gave me a cylindrical box of tin and taught me to recognize and gather a few of the commoner herbs and grasses. Or tried, rather, for even at five my mind was impervious to the facts of science and soon I carried sandwiches in my "botanising drum."

In the summer of my sixth year my father rented a house by a lake in Straussberg near Berlin. The village was still isolated. You took the train and then a stage-coach to reach it. There were swans on the lake and a boat, sheep in the meadows and goose-berry bushes in the garden. Over all a deep, brooding, old-world peace. My father employed weavers in the village and I saw them in their houses at the hand-looms. It was a city-child's first taste of country life. And the crow of a cock across the fields or the bleat of a sheep still brings to me a vision of the Brandenburg country-side. When we returned to Berlin I entered school and life became a grave and ordered matter.

II

Our home was a flat of seven rooms furnished with more solidity than grace. Beds, tables and chairs were of massive walnut and of a design so old-fashioned that I see it returning into favor. All these things had not been bought in shops. According to a sound, old custom even then, I suppose, on the wane, they had been made to order by a small master cabinetmaker. Here lived my father, my mother, my maternal grandmother and I. Nor must I forget the faithful, kindly Käthe who was with us and served us until that home was broken up. There entered into my perceptions, also, a janitor, his lank wife, their pale, blond children. But these remained remote and dim.

My people were Jews of unmixed blood and descent who had evidently lived for generations in the North and North East of Germany. I have before me now a picture of my grandfather taken in the sixties. Despite the fact that he performed rabbinical functions to scattered congregations in East Prussia, I observe that in contravention of the law, his face is clean-shaven and that he has no ear-locks; he is clad in the Western European fashion of his day. He was a large man with a liberal forehead, a humorous mouth and kindly eyes. From old, half-forgotten anecdotes I glean something of this character. He had much rabinnical learning, but a whimsical contempt for the ritual law; his familiar friends were the Protestant Pastor and the schoolmaster of the village; he was of frugal habits but of something dangerously like incompetence in worldly things. The power and intensity of the family belonged to my grandmother, who was much his junior and who survived him for over twenty years. It was she who had run the primitive little factory that turned cotton into wadding for the greatcoats needed in the severe winters on the Russian frontier; it was she who had toiled early and late that her sons might have an academic education. They were grateful to her and provided for her in her old age with a fine generosity. Of intimate tenderness to her they felt but little. She was a tall woman and a dour. She had strong practical sense but a tyrannical and gloomy temper. To me she melted, the only child of her youngest and of her only girl, and the memory touches me of her sitting on the green rep sofa, glasses on nose, and reading aloud to me the German fairy tales of which I never tired.

My father and mother were first cousins. Their racial and social origin was the same. So that I need not dwell on my paternal grand-parents of whom I know but little. The mother (my grandmother's sister) had died early. My grandfather had started out in life as a tanner, but had succeeded neither at his trade nor at anything else. I remember him well, for he was our guest on every Sunday. His white moustache and Vandyke beard gave him an air of false distinction, for his intelligence was limited and his manners clumsy. My mother treated him with gentleness, my father with a distant kindness. For my grandfather, being poor, had turned over his oldest child at the age of five to childless but wealthy relatives and this uncle and aunt had been, in the deeper sense, the only parents whom my father had ever known. From them, too, came the moderate but real prosperity that we enjoyed.

Other forms and faces are much clearer in my memory—a large circle of uncles and aunts and cousins, all acting with a special tenderness to me as the youngest child in the group. And chiefly I recall my mother's oldest and favorite brother. He was a man in the forties when I knew him, very tall and very stout. He was his mother's son. But her imperiousness and moroseness had been tempered in him by a fine and trained intelligence and by contact with men and with notable affairs. He had passed through the gymnasium at Insterburg and then studied law at Königsberg. Thrice he had fought for his country, in 1864, 1866 and 1870, and from the campaign in France he had returned with the iron cross. He had abandoned the law and occupied a distinguished position on the staff of a well-known Berlin newspaper. Punctilious and exacting and a tireless worker, he showed the kindlier elements of his nature in a wide hospitality and for many years his house in Berlin was the gathering place of the younger graduates of his Burschenschaft and his university. The letters which he wrote to my mother in America in the course of two decades I am glad to possess. The style is clear and expressive with a touch of austerity, the contents unaffectedly high-minded, melancholy (the badge of all our tribe) and warm-hearted.

This uncle had married a Gentile woman and for years the marriage was a stormy one. But his daughter, a fair, engaging girl somewhat older than I, was the companion and playmate of my earliest years, and the relations between my aunt and her Jewish kin were cordial and unclouded.

In truth, all the members of my family seemed to feel that they were Germans first and Jews afterwards. They were not disloyal to their race nor did they seek to hide it. Although they all spoke unexceptional High German they used many Hebrew expressions both among themselves and before their Gentile friends. But they had assimilated, in a deep sense, Aryan ways of thought and feeling. Their books, their music, their political interests were all German. I remember but one phrase disparaging to their Christian countrymen. It was a curious one: "What can one expect? The Gentile has no heart!"

Two scenes stand before me which symbolise the character of the social group from which I sprang. This is one: I am sitting in a half-darkened room and my heart beats and my cheeks burn. It is Christmas Eve. I look out through the dark pane and across the street. Ah, there, behind an uncurtained window, a tree with candles. Quickly I turn my eyes away. I do not want to taste the glory until it is truly mine. And at last, at last, a bell rings. The folding doors open and there—in the drawing room—stands my own tree in its glimmering splendor and around it the gifts from my parents and my grandmother and my uncles and aunts—charming German toys and books of fairytales and marchpane from Königsberg. And my mother takes me by the hand and leads me to the table and I feel as though I were myself walking straight into a fairytale . . .

And the other scene: It was my grandmother's custom, in pious remembrance of her husband, to visit the temple on the chief Jewish holidays—New Year and the Day of Atonement. And once, on the day of the great white fast, I was taken there to see her. The temple was large and rather splendid; the great seven-branched candelabra were of shining silver. The rabbi, the cantor and the large congregation of men were all clad in their gleaming shrouds and their white, silken praying shawls and had white caps on their heads. I can still see one venerable old man who read his Hebrew book through a large magnifying glass. The whiteness of the penitential scene was wonderful and solemn. Then the first star came out and the great day was over and in the vestibule I saw my grandmother being reverently saluted by her sons who wished her a happy holiday.

Two scenes. But the first was native and familiar to the heart of the child that I was: the second a little weird and terrifying and alien.

III

My father's foster-father was a man of some education and reading. Also an astute man who despite his severe lameness conducted a successful importing business from his armchair. His wife was a warm-hearted woman, but incurably erratic and had ended in hopeless madness when my father was a youth. It is clear that the adopted child received great kindness, was treated with indulgence or overindulgence, but never received any rational guidance. He was taken to France and Switzerland before he was fifteen, his ample allowance permitted him to satisfy his tastes in books and music and amateur scientific experimentation. But neither his mind nor his character underwent any discipline. Thus he grew up generous but wasteful. The bitter experience of later years corrected that fault. It could not correct his overeagerness, his lack of intellectual restraint, his habit of Utopian scheming, or the harsh self-assertiveness by which he strove to deaden his own sense of failure and insignificance. But neither could it impair his beautiful unselfishness and courage or his tireless devotion to the things of the mind. In later years I often found myself at variance with him in matters of opinion and belief; yet in face of his unfaltering devotion I was always consoled by the thought that I have scarcely a sound interest in literature or philosophy the impulse toward which had not come to me from his teaching and from his example . . .

He completed the course of the Royal Realschule at nineteen. He was too uncertain of himself to insist on prolonging his studies at the university; he already loved my mother and so he entered a well-known house of woolen manufacturers. By this time his foster-mother was hopelessly insane and his foster-father had fallen under the influence of an inferior woman. He had no real home. And so his request to be set up in business and to marry was readily granted. At twenty-three he was a father.

I often reflect upon his tragic youth. He was only a boy, crude, passionate, impulsive. He disliked his business but dared not slight it. Upon him were the eyes of my grandmother and of my mother's brothers. Their scrutiny, I am afraid, was more severe than sympathetic. The society in which he lived placed great stress on dignity and seemliness of demeanor. And so he tried hard to play the man and the man of business. That, under these circumstances, he escaped obvious disaster for eight years bears witness to his feeling of duty and his endurance.

My earliest recollections of him are all of his hours of escape from drudgery and care. He would sit in the mellow gas-light of our sitting-room and read far into the night. Or I would wake up and see him in the adjoining room, reading in bed by candle-light. And on cold or rainy Sundays and holidays he would spend hours and hours at the piano. He played most imperfectly at best, but he read his scores accurately and with fine musical intelligence and his halting technique did not prevent him from hearing all the grace and charm of Mozart, all the loftiness and solemn sweetness of Beethoven . . .

My mother did not come to Berlin until her father died. She was then only twelve years old. But a deep and tenacious loyalty attached her to the bleak East Prussian village of her childhood, and for years she was never weary of telling, nor I of hearing, stories of those early days. Thus I know how the intense, dark-eyed little girl with the very red cheeks of a northern climate hastened, wrapped in a heavy shawl, through the snowy dusk to afternoon school, clutching a candle with which to light her form. Or how, on other days, she went eagerly to the house of a superannuated spinster who had been a governess in gentlemen's families to learn French and crocheting and tatting. She brought from that old home, moreover, a fine heritage of folk-songs and tales and sayings. Much that I learned from her lips as early as I learned anything I have found since in the collections of folklorists and students of popular poetry and song. She was all her life, despite her Jewishness, her wide and sad experience and her artistic tastes, a spiritual child of the German folk. A hundred times, when her hair was white and her heart worn with sorrow and disappointment, I have seen in her eyes, in her whole self arise suddenly a ghostly but sweet shadow of the sturdy East-Prussian lass—simple and deep-hearted and of the very soul of her homeland.

Her education in Berlin was old-fashioned and limited. It was long before the days of the gymnasium for girls. Yet within its narrow range the Höhere

Töchterschule had thoroughness. My mother's knowledge of French, at least, was sound and extensive. Her chief interest, however, in those days, was music. Her alto voice was well cultivated. When I awoke to the consciousness of art I found that I knew—and could remember no time at which I had not known— the words and music of practically all the great songs of Schubert and Schumann, of Franz and Mendelssohn and Brahms. So often, during my childhood, had I heard them from her lips.

Her girlhood was not happy. The social environment was cruelly rigid; one breathed according to law. She wanted to enter a seminary for teachers; she begged to be allowed to learn book-keeping. But since there was no need, her brothers decided that it was unseemly for a young woman to work outside of the home. When the dusk stole into the small Berlin flat and she was weary of music and embroidery, she would go out in all weathers and hurry through the streets and let the rain beat upon her face—intensely troubled, rebellious against the forces that held her. Yet she was quite helpless. For her strength never lay in nimbleness of mind; neither then nor later did she reflect closely; it lay in the fullness and richness of her emotional nature. But she had been carefully taught to distrust her impulses. She wrote verses and dared not show them. Even so she was considered unconventional and shrank more and more within herself. She entertained a deep affection for a young pianist through whom she caught glimpses of a freer life. But he was hopelessly poor and drifted away. She received the most intelligent sympathy, after all, from her young cousin, my father. They read the same books, loved the same music, nursed their enthusiasm on the same plays. He was reputed, moreover, to be the heir of a very large fortune. Neither knew that his foster-father, as a matter of fact, had lost many thousands in the financial collapse that followed the inflation of the early seventies. And she thought, quite rightly, that money means liberty in the higher and finer as well as in the coarser and more obvious sense.

Once married, however, my father's crudeness and violence wore on her; a moroseness in him which was the result of the harsh pressure which he endured and would not admit, estranged her. Again she was baffled and solitary. Then her child was born. The tension snapped. Into the channel of her maternal love she poured all her passionate ideality, all her deep yearning, all her half-inarticulate ambitions, all the splendor of her frustrate hopes. In the wild and tragic munificence of her love she kept nothing for herself. Utterly she transferred the centre of her being to another. It was wrong! Wrong to herself. The world is wide and its paths are many and the fate of no man is quite his own to shape. So that through my failures and misfortunes and enforced wanderings her life was again beggared and often darkened. I loved her and I mourn her with all my strength. Yet to her great love I was—as any man would have been—but an unprofitable servant.

IV

My life until I went to school was an intense waking dream. The pretty toys I had interested me but little. I shrank from playmates not through timidity but because they interrupted my imaginings. Their amusements seemed aimless and their noise made me feel sick and faint. Yet I was by no means a delicate child; I was sturdy and broad-chested and passed vigorously through two rather severe illnesses that attacked me early. But just as the taste of certain dainties that I liked gave me a pleasure that was almost too keen, so disagreeable sense-impressions made me dizzy and, on at least one occasion, violently ill. An old aunt had died and my mother took me with her on a visit of condolence. The room was full of black-garbed women; there was a faint stale odor of flowers and a continuous buzz of conversation. It all seemed hideous to me; I fainted and had to be carried home. The only child whom I admitted to full intimacy was my fair-haired cousin. She was musical, her voice was soft, her ways with me were gentle. I loved to touch the fine texture of her skin and the silkiness of her long hair. Curiously enough I cannot remember how, in those earliest years, we entertained each other. I recall with the utmost vividness that I thought her lovely, and that the sight of her touched me like the lilacs of spring or the sound of singing ...

Most of my waking dreams have vanished from my mind. But two I entertained so constantly and so long that I remember them as though they had been realities. I imagined a great garden in an endless summer. In it were gathered under cool groves the few people whom I loved. There were tables under the trees laden with things to eat—roast duck and Baumkuchen and clusters of large, cool, translucent grapes. A Never-Never land. The other dream was more boyish.

A FAR CHILDHOOD

I saw myself, clad in green huntman's garb, a cock's feather in my hat, riding swiftly on a small, lithe horse. Whither or why? I don't know. That vision of myself was enough and was a source of endless delight.

When I was four years old I was sent to a Kindergarten. But I was so obviously unhappy and listless that the principal asked my mother to keep me at home. Then my grandmother taught me my letters and my real life began. My first two books were collections of stories written for little children and I thought them delightful. But someone brought me a small, greenish volume bound in boards. It was called Bechstein's Märchen. Faded and tattered the little book lies before me as I write. I turn the pages—to this day I know them almost by heart—I look at the small, stiff, quaint, inimitably haunting wood-cuts. . . . Immemorial romance, sombre and magical world of dim forests and mediaeval cities and doomed kings, of shepherds and gnomes, full of old racial memories, free as the imagination of childhood, deep as the heart of man! The style, I see now, was worthy of the matter—concrete, marrowy, quaint as the wood-cuts with flashes now and then, of a wild, grotesque humor . . . For the first time in my life I became insistent, begging for books and more books. Thus I read Grimm and Andersen for myself now and the Arabian Nights and a large and precious volume called Al-Runa in which were gathered fairy-tales of all peoples—German and English and Norse, Romaic and Russian and the weird and cruel legends of the Southern Slavs. I read until my eyes ached and my forehead was fevered. If my mother bade me go and play in the open I lay on the door-step without and wept in a passion of despair. No wonder! I have lived with books and loved the best things in more than one literature. Yet what has the highest delight of later years been to that pure and passionate joy, that ecstasy of absorption in which I became one with the things I read and saw with my own eyes castles by the shores of Norseland, dragons on the banks of lustrous rivers and with my own ears heard the blowing of the horns of Elfland. . . .

My condition was, of course, an unhealthy one, and my mother dealt with it energetically. On four afternoons a week I was sent to the Tiergarten in charge of a young Kindergärtnerin, on other afternoons my mother took long walks with me, a habit which we continued for many years. I said that she dealt with this matter energetically. But not with this alone. Her love was no ignoble indulgence. It held no element of moral sloth. My diet was determined by the family physician, not by my liking. For every time I tasted sweets or pastry, an American child of to-day tastes them a hundred times. I slept on a pillow of horsehair; I used not the traditional feather-bed but the hardier blanket. . . . It never occurred to me that I could fail to obey my father and mother; it never occurred to my cousin and the other children whom we knew that they could fail to obey theirs. Thus between parents and young children the relations were far more dignified and becoming, far more fruitful of a fine piety than any I have seen since. There may have been an occasional injustice. We are all human. There was no noise, no wrangling, no vulgar antagonism. . . . After the care of my body, my mother's love took the form of an intense and glowing ambition for me. I was to realize my highest possibilities, to develop every faculty, to attain every ability and grace that mark the complete man. I learned skating in winter and swimming in summer, always under competent instruction. I was taught music and gymnastics. I have heard mothers complain with a certain wistfulness that it was time for their children to go to school. I have seen them put off the evil day. My mother with her German ideals felt altogether differently. With almost an austerity of joy she welcomed the autumn of my sixth year. The great process of development was now to begin in earnest. The day was a solemn day for her. Consciously she now dedicated herself to a double watchfulness, helpfulness and devotion during the momentous years that were to come.

V

The society into which I was born, whatever were its virtues or its faults, had one notable quality: it knew what it wanted. A few aims and their implied values were fixed. The kind of school I was to attend was never debated. It was an absolutely foregone conclusion that a liberal education was the necessary foundation of right and noble living. My parents were of modest origin and of modest means. But if anyone had questioned my being prepared for the gymnasium and proceeding from thence to the university, they would have held it a prophecy of my early death. My uncles entertained the same feeling concerning their sons, and among the painful memories of my childhood is the gray, tragic face of one of them whose boy had that day failed to pass his Reifeprüfung. So deeply

did this conviction, which was considered beyond discussion, sink into my consciousness that, to this day,
the debate concerning the value of a higher education
so often heard among us in America, has no more
real content for me than a debate concerning the value
of bread. . . .

The gymnasium which admitted me to its Vorschule
was housed in an ancient building, four stories high,
constructed of heavy and rather gloomy stones. I do
not know where it was. I know that on my way to
school I passed one house that was almost hidden by
roses in the spring, and that I passed a handsome new
church that stood in a small, green square. The
wooden stairs of the gaunt, old schoolhouse were
deeply worn by the steps of generations of boys and
youths, the yard was bleak and paven, the rooms light
but barren of any adornment; the forms were dark-
brown with splashes of ink.

During the first week at school I learned to know
loneliness and homesickness and began to develop,
too, a certain quiet stoicism which staid with me for
many years and did me measureless harm. The
teacher, a lank, kindly man with a long, blond beard,
left the room for a little. He found it in uproar when
he returned. I had been quiet. But I, too, felt the
smarting taps of his cane across my shoulders. I did
not cry and I did not tell my mother until years later.
It was the only punishment I received at the school
during the two years of my attendance. Soon this
very teacher singled me out with much kindness, visited our home when I was ill with a heavy cold and
commended me to the teacher who followed him. By
this time too, I had made friends of several of my little

fellow-pupils and the first wretched feeling of forlor-
ness had worn off.

The instruction was simple in its subject-matter:
reading, writing, arithmetic, singing, gymnastics and
"religion." I know now that it was remarkably thorough. I am hopelessly stupid at figures. For six
weary years at high school and college I dragged my
numb mind through five or, at the best, three periods
of mathematical instruction a week. I could not tell
now, literally to save my life, the nature of a quad-
ratic equation. But I know the elementary arithmetic
learned in that German school. I don't need to multi-
ply simple figures, for instance. I know the answers
instinctively and at once. . . . The hour I liked best
was that known as "religion" As a Jew I could easily
have been excused from attending. But my parents
had no prejudices in this respect. And they were right.
For there was no hint of dogma, not even of moralizing. The teacher simply related to us the Old Testa-
ment legends in chronological order, and to me it
seemed as though I heard a new and fascinating set of
fairy-tales. I had a vision of the tower of Babel piercing a tropic sky, of long lines of camels under solemn
stars, of tall, dark maidens carrying pitchers to ancient
wells by the tents of Jacob. . . .

The home-work was harder. My mother's intense
ambition for me made her severe. She bought a desk
for me which stood, as did its chair, on a little wooden
platform several feet in height. While I sat at this desk
she could, small as I was, stand beside me. And so we
worked together until my tasks were perfectly done—
until I had written my copy-book page and could recite
my verses without hesitation. These tasks, I think,

grew longer than was quite wise during my second year at school. I shed some childish tears of weariness, I know, and my mother grew a little anxious over my lack of zeal.

But life was not all work. There was the magic of Christmas and Easter with generous vacations; there was the delight of spring with flower-girls on the curb. I had an allowance of one mark a week now and spent most of it on posies for my mother and my blond cousin. Above all, in winter there was an occasional visit to a theatrical performance of some fairy play—a pleasure almost too rich and keen to be quite free from pain. Also there were children's parties. But I cared less for these than for a quiet afternoon with one of my fellows at school—a little lad of almost girlish delicacy and of my own tastes. And there were long walks with my mother, and skating in winter with my cousin and summer outings. . . . A rich and happy childhood. Even my grandmother's death darkened it only for a week or two. Nor, in my childish preoccupations, did I hear the mutterings that preceeded the final crash of our prosperity and our hopes.

VI

Years afterwards I learned, of course, all the disheartening details of my father's financial ruin. They would make but a dull story. Late in the year 1889 his foster-father died and left him about twenty thousand dollars, the remnant of a once considerable fortune. With this sum he rashly engaged in an undertaking of which he knew nothing—the importation of Italian fruits. He paid an exorbitant sum for the good-will of a worthless firm, for lighters that did not exist, for customers that could not be found. In three months he was ruined and, overcome by shame and despair, fell ill. His illness was not of the body. It was a slight attack of melancholia. The psychical inhibitions were, of course, paralysing. Yet no one, not even his physician, quite understood that fact. He was urged to see friends and former associates, to seek a position here and there. But it was impossible for him to face the world. Aimlessly he wandered about and reported (and probably believed) that he had met only coldness and rebuffs. My mother, not dreaming that his mind was sick, credited these reports; they shook her faith in men and increased her fundamental self-distrust. Thus in the midst of friends and kinsmen who would, in the traditional Jewish fashion, have scolded loudly but helped generously, my father and mother were isolated, embittered and helpless. . . .

A day came which I have never forgotten. My father and mother stood in our living room. A shaft of September sunshine fell upon them both. My father held his hand to his mouth; one of his delusions was that his tongue was slightly paralysed; my mother turned the pages of a letter. Her eyes rested on him in sorrow and perplexity Suddenly she spoke: "Would you like to go to America?" My father drew himself up. A strange and almost unnatural relief came into his face. "Yes," he gasped. Then he turned to me with the first smile he had worn in weeks. "Would you like to go to America, to Uncle S.?"

Long before, the youngest of my mother's four brothers had emigrated to America. He was said to have prospered moderately there. The letter was from him. The relief which my father had shown was followed by a fever of activity. Though his life had been, however rash and foolish, of an unblemished honor, he councilled my mother to secrecy. She blamed herself bitterly in later years for having followed his council. He was like a man trying to flee from himself.

Weeks of turmoil followed. I felt keenly the hidden terror and the loud confusion. My father was possessed by the morbid notion that he himself would have to carry all our luggage. He sold our furniture, his excellent library; with difficulty my mother saved the silver and linen and my books. . . . It was autumn and it rained and rained. My mother felt a thousand hesitations. Again and again she was on the point of speaking out, of appealing to her brothers. Pride and self-distrust and my father's sudden, diseased energy constrained her. Then, one day, the tickets had been bought and, with a very ache of tragic foreboding, she faced an accomplished fact. Deep in her heart she nursed one bleak consolation. The two thousand dollars with which my father intended to start life in America were in her keeping. Whatever happened she determined to cling to enough for our return passage. . . .

Hamburg! I shall never forget it, though I was but a child of eight. A sky of slate, an angry wind, ancient streets with tall, gabled mediaeval houses leading to a square, the stuffy hotel full of horse-hair covered chairs and sofas, the sad-faced man who exchanged German money for American, the broad Elbe river and the fog-horns of the tugs and ferries. The fog-horns . . . I stop writing and listen. Beyond the park, close by the river, the train comes in. Its whistle blows a hoarse blast. Straightway—it never fails—thirty years are swept away, I am in Hamburg again, proud of my long great-coat, filled with a strange sense, half of expectancy, half of terror, wondering at the whiteness of my mother's face and the unspeakable wistfulness in her eyes. . . .

At ten in the forenoon we boarded the ferry that was to take us to our ship. It was the old Hamburg-American liner Suevia. She carried only first-class passengers and steerage. We were among the former. The trip took several hours, I believe, but I am not sure. Then the great ship received us and to me it immediately became a world of wonder. At luncheon I marvelled at the array of wine and water glasses hanging like chandeliers above the tables, at the swivel chairs fastened to the floor, at the strange sounds on the lips of other passengers. "They are speaking English," my father said to me.

Dark fell; the ship was in motion; my father paced the deck, up and down, up and down. At last a shattering doubt of this adventure had come into his mind. My mother stood by the railing. She held my hand in a convulsive grasp and covered me with the cape of her long coat. The tears rolled down her cheeks as the twinkle of the last shore-lights died and nothing was left but darkness of the land she was not to see again.

CHAPTER II

THE AMERICAN SCENE

I

The Suevia, scheduled to reach New York on the ninth day, did not arrive until the fifteenth. Not a fleck of sunshine all those days; a sky almost black, a piping wind, a turbulent sea dashing up in huge steel-gray waves with bottle-green under-curves and fierce, white, fang-like edges. A primaeval, chaotic, brutal sea. The great ship quivered and creaked and wheezed; the water slapped against the port-holes and ran down the round, dim panes; almost hourly the propeller was punched clear above sea-level and whirred with a naked, metallic grind. . . . My mother was hopelessly sea-sick the whole time; my father and I led a dim, nebulous existence, when possible on deck, when not, in the red-carpeted saloon. But the sea got hold of the innermost core of my mind; it became part of my life, and in inland places I have often caught myself tense with desire after its tang and roar.

Our land-fall was still gray but quiet. Afar off lay a dim, hook-like shore. The voyage had liberated my father's mind from terror and madness. He was so strengthened and cheered that even my mother smiled. To come to land at all seemed, after our tremendous experience, almost like coming home. But the pier at Hoboken was rough and wild, a place of hoarse cries and brute haste and infernal confusion. A kindly German-American fellow-passenger helped us; saw to it that our luggage was not unduly searched and put us in a rumbling hack on our way to an hotel. It was Meyer's Hotel, a comfortable, unpretentious place. We were worn out and rested well during our first night on American soil under the strange mosquito-bars.

The place where my uncle lived and whither we were bound lay far away in the South Atlantic States. But my father and mother thought that we ought to rest for a day or two and see a city so great and famous as New York. A curious timidity kept us, however, from venturing far through the grime and rattle. We crossed the Brooklyn Bridge, I know, and saw the gilt dome of the World Building, then the tallest structure on this hemisphere, and the elevated railroad. But we did not go up town nor into the financial section, drifted somehow into a lake of mud shaken by trucks and drays on Canal Street and retreated to Hoboken.

Being ill-advised we took ship again and spent nearly fifty hours on a coast-wise voyage South. We could eat no food. Negro stewards served it and over it was the strange flavor of bananas and Concord grapes. There was no storm or gloom now. But the brilliantly radiant sea was rough and choppy and the steamer small. The weather grew milder and milder and when we steamed into Queenshaven harbor the day was like spring.

The bay is one of the most beautiful in the world. In its fold lies the old city with its gardens and veran-

dahs and its few slender spires. Golden-green islands
extend its curves. The coloring of sea and sky, in
whatever mood, is of so infinite and delicate a variety
as though the glow and splendor of all the jewels in
the world had been melted there. And over city and
bay lies a rich quietude that steals upon the heart
through the liquid softness of that untroubled air. I
heard my father and mother speak of the beauty of the
scene; my own sense of it must have been vague. But
I cannot disassociate that early vision from an hundred later ones. For that city and bay came to mean
my boyhood and youth, high passion and aspiration,
and later a grief that darkened my life. I close my
eyes: I can see every stone of the old city, every wave
of the bay. But my mind sees both garbed in a cruel
and unearthly sweetness. My bodily eyes could endure
to see neither of them any more. . . . Friends of my
uncle who were commissioned to meet us missed the
boat. My father summoned his scraps of English,
hired a four-wheeler and took us to the Queenshaven
Hotel. There these people found us, astonished that
my parents had not yet acquired the habits of poverty
but had gone boldly to the best hotel in the city. They
took us to their house where the children astonished me
by speaking English. It did not seem to me nearly
so curious in grown persons. I stared at the tattered
Negroes in the yard, almost too tired to be impressed
by any strangeness. In the afternoon our friends took
us to our train, shoved us into a day-coach and hurried off.

I recall vividly the long, shabby, crowded car and
its peculiar reek of peanuts, stale whiskey and chew-
ing-tobacco. Half of the passengers were burly ne-

groes who gabbled and laughed weirdly. The white men wore broad-rimmed wool-hats, whittled and spat and talked in drawling tones. I very distinctly shared my parents' sense of the wildness, savagery and roughness of the scene, their horrified perception of its contrast to anything they had ever known or seen. Soon the dark fell and at the wayside stations queer, pan-like lamps flared up in reddish ribbands of fire. At one station a group of men entered carrying tall cudgels. They opened jack-knives and proceeded to peel and devour these cudgels. My mother grew almost hysterical; my father racked his mind and discovered some half-forgotten information on the subject of sugar-cane. . . . At ten o'clock we reached Saint Mark's and trudged out of the car. A man with heavy moustaches and clad in a red sweater lifted me from the platform. From my previous experience of life I judged him to be a porter or a cabby. To my disgust and amazement he called me by name and kissed me on the mouth. It was my uncle.

II

In 1890 the village of St. Mark's in South Carolina was raw; it had more than a touch of wildness and through its life there ran a strain of violence. It consisted of two principal streets, running diagonally to each other and of half a dozen lesser streets that trailed off into cotton-fields and pine-forests. There was a cotton-seed oil mill, a saw mill and twenty to thirty general merchandise stores. Three or four of these were housed in one-story buildings of red brick. For the rest the village was built of wood and many of the houses were unpainted, showing the browned and weather-beaten boards. There was a Methodist Church and a Baptist Church, each with a grave-yard behind it. North of the village straggled a Negro grave-yard, its graves decorated with colored pebbles, bits of iridescent glass and the broken shards of cheap vases. Here and there, behind houses or in chance lanes were small, black, one-roomed huts inhabited by Negro women. These women were in domestic service in the village and, as I learned later, plied, in addition and quite openly, an equally ancient but less honest trade. Despite eight or ten bar-rooms the streets were quiet except on Saturday. Then the village flared into life. Many hundreds of Negroes came in from the sparsely settled country; they rode in on horses or mules or oxen or drove rough carts and primitive wagons, and were themselves generally clad in garments of which the original homespun had disappeared in a mass of gaudy patches. They traded and drank and, child-like, spent their money on foolish things— perfumes and handsome whips and sweets. Toward dusk they reeled in a hot turmoil and filled the air with that characteristic odor of peanuts and stale whiskey and chewing tobacco.

I watched the village life with a deep sense of its strangeness but almost without astonishment. Soon I was merged into it and felt quite at home. No, not quite. During at least a year, at lengthening intervals of course, I felt a sharp nostalgia for the land of my birth and its life. Suddenly, at the edge of the forest, a sense of grief would overcome me. Somewhere beyond those dark trees, beyond leagues of country, beyond the ocean, lay our home. . . . And I would weep bitterly. And still, in my maturer years the edge of a forest or else a few solitary trees at a great distance bring back to me that old sense of wistfulness and yearning—no longer for definite scenes or associations, but for the mystery of delight I have not known, beauty I have not seen, peace I have sought in vain. . . .

The Southern country-side awakened in me, child that I was, a rich, an almost massive joy in nature. About a mile beyond the lonely little railroad station with its bales of cotton and acrid-smelling sacks of yellow guano lay the "red hills." These hills were not very high; I could climb them easily; they were covered with very tall, very straight pine-trees that seemed to me shaft-like and sky-piercing. Through a fold of the hills ran a rapid, very shallow little brook over a bed of clean, bright pebbles. In spring the dogwood showed its white blossoms there; in the mild Southern autumn a child could lie on the deep layers of brownish pine-needles and play with the aromatic cones and gaze up at the brilliant blue of the sky.

The summer stirred me deeply. I had been used to the cool, chaste, frugal summers of the North. Here the heat smote; the vegetation sprang into rank and hot luxuriance—noisome weeds with white ooze in their stems and bell-like pink flowers invaded the paths and streets. I felt a strange throbbing, followed by sickish languor and a dumb terror at the frequent, fierce thunderstorms. Both my intelligence and my instincts ripened with morbid rapidity and I attribute many abnormalities of temper and taste that are mine to that sudden transplantation into a semi-tropical world. . . .

I was a thorough child nevertheless and delighted

in certain acquisitions which the new world brought me—a percussion cap pistol, a mouth organ, a Jew's harp. Nor did I give up my old life. My books had been saved and, one day, my father discovered that he had forgotten a small balance in the Deutsche Bank. For this money he ordered books from Germany, and I came into possession of a set of very red volumes: the marvelous chap-books of the Reformation age— Griseldis, Genoveva, Robert the Devil, Dr. Faustus— naive and knightly or magical and grim; and of two slimmer volumes called Beckers Erzählungen aus der Alten Welt, which contained the Iliad and the Odyssey in simple, lucid German prose. In the reading of these, especially of the Odyssey, culminated the imaginative joys of my childhood. I do not know Greek; I cannot read Homer in the original. Yet I am sure that I know what Homer is. In a plain room behind the store in which apples and cloth and furniture and plough- shares and rice and tinned fish were sold to chatter- ing Negroes, I sat with my book and clearly heard

"The surge and thunder of the Odyssey"

and saw Nausikaa and her maidens, white limbed and fair, on the shore of the wine-dark sea, and dwelt with Odysseus on the island of Callypso and returned home with him to Ithaca—not without tears—and listened to the twanging bow-string that sped the avenging ar- rows. The wood-cut that was the frontispiece of the little volume showed Hermes on his mission of com- mand to Circe. Above floats the god with his staff and his winged cap and sandals. Below him stretches the immeasurable stream of ocean. In the back- ground, small and far but very clear, lies an island with a tiny fane of Doric columns. I gazed at the picture for hours and knew the freshness, the grace and the clarity of that morning of the world.

III

My uncle and aunt received us into their queer little house which was huddled, as though for protection, against the shop. The walls of the house were of the rudest; the wind blew through knot-holes in the timber. My father and mother were bitterly disappointed. My uncle had sent the St. Mark's Herald to Berlin and my father, who did not understand the art and vocabulary of town-booming nor the society items of an American village newspaper, assumed that St. Mark's was a town of some importance and my uncle a prominent citizen. And here he had come to a squalid village, the guest of a man well-enough liked by his fellow citizens but wretchedly poor. My aunt, moreover, though a woman of some kindly qualities, was a Jewess of the Eastern tradition, narrow-minded, given over to the clattering ritual of pots and pans— "meaty" and "milky"—and very ignorant. On the very evening of our arrival, having at last withdrawn to the one spare bed-room, my father and mother looked blankly at each other. A chill wind blew in thin, keen streams through chinks in the bare, wooden wall, the geese squawked loudly in the muddy yard, my aunt was heard scolding her little girls in a mixture of Yiddish and English, a little, unshaded kerosene lamp made the grim room look all the gloomier. My mother sat down on the springless bed, a picture of desolation. The sudden plunge unnerved her. All through the voyage we had lived on our accustomed plane of civilized comfort. Only here did the descent begin.

She had one consolation that apparently justified the whole adventure. My father was a changed man. From now on and for many years he was full of energy and buoyancy, splendidly patient and brave, always ready to cheer her in her fits of loneliness and depression. He had shaken off the morbid inhibitions and immediately started out into the village to see what he could do.

The people of the village, storekeepers, a few retired farmers, three physicians, three or four lawyers, came of various stocks—English, Scotch-Irish, German, even French and Dutch. But they were all descended from early nineteenth century settlers and had become thorough Americans. Everybody belonged to either the Baptist or the Methodist church. The Methodists were, upon the whole, more refined, had better manners than the Baptists and were less illiterate. Among all the villagers there was a moderate amount of hard drinking and a good deal of sexual irregularity, especially with Mulatto women. I have since wondered that there was not more. The life was sterile and monotonous enough. They were all kindly, even the rougher ones, not very avaricious, no drivers of hard bargains, given to talking about shooting but doing very little of it. (During the two years of our residence two men were shot and in each case upon extreme provocation.) Also so far as their light went, they were liberal. This was well illustrated by the position of the Jews in the village. Of these there were about ten families, all recent immigrants, and so aliens in speech and race and faith. Most of them, moreover, were quite prosperous. Yet between them and these Southern villagers the relations were hearty and pleasant and consolidated by mutual kindness and tolerance. Only one Jew and that was my father, was looked upon with some suspicion by the severer among his Gentile neighbors. The reason was curious and significant; he did not perform the external rites of the Jewish faith and, upon entering a fraternal life insurance order, he smiled and hesitated when asked to affirm categorically his belief in a personal God.

He soon saw that there was nothing to be done in St. Mark's except add another to the existing shops. But since nearly every one seemed to have prospered and since the quiet and the easy, democratic atmosphere of the place appealed to him, he hesitated but little. Help and good advice were offered alike by Jew and Gentile and, at the end of a few months, we were installed in some pleasant rooms beside one of the few brick stores on Main Street. There was the usual heterogeneous stock of food and implements, furniture and dry-goods. My mother went to Queenshaven and bought adequate furniture for our little home.

Although she yearned very bitterly for her native land, her friends and kin, for music and for all the subtle supports of the civilization in which she was so deeply rooted, life opened fairly enough. Domestic service cost next to nothing, food was plentiful and cheap. Even friends were not wanting. Our landlord and his family, prominent members of the Methodist church, saw soon enough that my father and mother were of a different mental type and of different antecedents from the other Jews in St. Mark's. There followed an exchange of visits. Mrs. C. gave my mother much good advice, explained to her many American ways and manners that seemed very strange, and tried to console her in regard to her most burning and immediate problem—that of my education. This friendship led to others. And so when summer came, we who had no vegetable garden—and would have been just as helpless had we had one—received daily attentions from our Gentile friends: baskets of tomatoes or okra or sweet-corn or bell-pepper. And one friend, a very aged physician who liked and admired my mother and had a dim but steady perception of her profound spiritual isolation, sent her weekly a great basketful of roses. My father, at the same time, found a congenial companion in a young lawyer. The two played chess together and from him my father borrowed Shakespeare and Byron, Dickens and Thackeray and Scott with whose works he was, like all educated Germans, thoroughly familiar and whom he now read with avidity in their own language. We saw a good deal of my uncle and his family and their friends. But culturally we really felt closer to the better sort of Americans in the community, and so there began in those early days that alienation from my own race which has been the source to me of some good but of more evil.

IV

I do not know how I learned English. My memory which is so clear on things quite trivial fails me at this crucial point. My mother characteristically desired to engage a teacher for me. And for this purpose my uncle introduced the Baptist minister of the village. At the end of one lesson, however, of which

my memory is most faint, the Reverend Mr. Crossland declared that far better results could be obtained
if I were to attend his school. This advice was followed and my next memory, in the matter of language,
shows me in my little German velvet suit and cap
seated aloft on sacks of cotton-seed in the postmas-
ter's shop and explaining, in some sort of English,
the peculiarities of German life to a crowd of tall,
rough tobacco-spitting but evidently tender-hearted
yokels. Tender-hearted! For they asked the quaint
little German boy to come again and again and never
teased him but were, in what must have been their
amusement, unfailingly gentle and considerate.

There was no public school in St. Mark's in my
time. And so the Baptist congregation had built a
school-house of rough unpainted timber on a barren
field beside the church. Here Crossland and one young
woman, in a single gaunt room, taught about an hundred boys and girls, ranging in age from seven to
seventeen. Some of the children came a distance of
ten miles to school and to every available tree were
tethered Texas ponies or mules, some saddled, some
hitched to road-carts or buggies. Details that stand
out in my memory are the sombre glow of the cast-
iron stove on cold days, the plaintive notes of some
birds circling over the little Baptist grave-yard, the
hair—yellow as wheat—and the brilliantly white teeth
of one of the older girls. And two things inspired in
me a vague sense of fear: the switches with which the
Reverend Mr. Crossland occasionally beat the boys'
legs and the old cigar-box, filled with earth, into which
he spat amazing streams of repulsive brown juice.
Sometimes he would order a boy to empty and refill

[45]

this box and I lived in terror of being singled out for this office. I never was. But the existence of this box, betrayed in one of my rare moments of talkativeness, astonished my parents so overwhelmingly that they forthwith removed me from the school.

My relations to my fellow-pupils were slight. There was much friendliness on both sides, but a dreamy, childish absorption kept me solitary. I am certain of only this: that I was reprimanded for steadily abandoning the boys' side of the play-ground during recess and losing myself among the girls. They were gentler and aroused in me a faint, impersonal perception of comeliness. . . .

The village possessed one other school which charged a somewhat higher fee—two dollars a month, I think— and boasted an aristocratic flavor. It was kept by a broken-down gentleman of Huguenot extraction who was said to have been immensely wealthy and to have lived in a state of barbaric splendor before the Civil War. Major Maury was a man prematurely old, slightly deaf and shaken by palsy. His features were almost hidden by harsh bunches of beard, and hair grew in long strands out of his ears and nostrils. He sat by a window, smoking a pipe and chewing tobacco at the same time. There, in a weary, mechanical way, he heard the lessons which we were supposed to have prepared in the other bare rooms or on the porch of the windy and abandoned cottage. The ten or twelve pupils played and studied around that sunken-eyed old man in a half-hearted kind of way; the manner and the mood of the place float to me across the years in images of chill discouragement and mouldering desolation.

But by this time my mother, with the energy which marked those early days, had acquired a considerable English vocabulary and had taken council of her friend Mrs. C. She removed me from Major Maury's "academy" and proceeded to prepare me for entrance to the High School of Queenshaven. It was a fine and brave action. She had been in America less than a year; her pronunciation was very imperfect; she had to teach me with a German-English dictionary in hand. Yet my days of mere dreamy loitering were over and I have never had instruction more accurate or solid. We had Appleton's Fifth Reader, Smith's English Grammar, Noah Webster's Speller, a geography and an arithmetic. I have not seen those books since, but I can visualize many of their pages to this day.

In the reader I came upon my first fragments of English literature: Addison's Vision of Mirza, Childe Harold's Farewell To His Native Land, and The Death of Absalom, by Nathaniel Parker Willis. I felt even then that the last piece was clumsy and rhetorical, nor did Byron touch me; Addison's fable seemed exquisite—as, indeed, it is—and I read it over and over. . . . But stronger and coarser food for my childish mind was at hand in the English books which now came to me and which I evidently read with an entire absence of effort. The first was, by a queer chance, The Swiss Family Robinson. I recognized its inferiority to my familiar German versions of Crusoe and Gulliver, but its strange blending of the exotic and the matter of fact drew me on and I sedulously skipped the moralizing. . . . At the same time, however, there was given me a set of yellowish, paper-backed books. I recall the title of but one: Tom

Tracy, The Newsboy. These were books of the Horatio Alger type, but better done, I think, and not so stereotyped. They took possession of my mind by a strong and coarse compulsion. For I had been nursed upon beauty. The clearness and grace of the Homeric world, the pageantry of the Middle Age, islands in the tropic seas at the ends of the earth—these were possessions of my imagination. And so these tales of New York boys who were "manly" and "got on" seemed to me of an overwhelming reality. The hideous moral utilitarianism, the vulgar confusion of values in these books passed, of course, entirely over my head. I didn't want to get on; I hadn't a spark of ambition; I never thought or prattled, as many children do, of what I would be when I grew up. I read these books, at the age of ten, with the same sense of deeply satisfied absorption in the fine, narrowy realities of life with which, at the end of another decade, I first read Vanity Fair and Mme. Bovary.

V

Suddenly, upon a day amid the steady radiance of that Southern summer a blind, imperious impulse took hold of me. Though always clumsy with my hands and careless of manual skill, I hastened into our little yard, gathered some abandoned boxes and built me a rude, shaky little desk. It was too high to sit at. So I stood and wrote—for the first time—verse and prose: tales of disaster at sea, of ultimate islands, of peaceless wandering. The prose and verse were mixed indiscriminately, assonance sufficed in place of rime, all I felt was an intense inner glow. It was all instinctively done in German. And I emphasize this fact in the development of an American since that childish outburst marked the first and last time on which I used my original mother-tongue in writing as a matter of course and without a sense of deliberately limiting such powers of expression as I may have. . . . That first impulse lasted, with daily but decreasing passion, for some weeks. Then it died out. I neither wondered nor regretted it. To me it was a solitary game, and most of my amusements were solitary. Perhaps the shifting from one language to another caused this, perhaps a momentous change in my inner life which now took place.

Our friend, Mrs. C., was a very fervent member of her church. She was too well bred to engage in crude proselytising. But, seeing that we observed no Jewish rites, she suggested that it would improve my English if I were to join her Sunday School class. My mother who had precious memories of snow-swept Christmas services in her native East Prussian village, made no objection. My father, an agnostic reared on Huxley and Haeckel, had no prejudices for or against any religious cult. The question was settled much more smoothly than, I imagine, Mrs. C. had hoped. She was intensely interested in her new pupil, yet her interest was never tactless or obtrusive. I have grown infinitely far away from her teaching; I have nothing but kindness for her memory.

The small, white church with its wooden belfry was like a thousand others. It stood in a sun-flooded street, behind it were scattered graves and then cotton fields running to olive or brownish pine-forests. The calm of the village Sundays was truly sabbatical and the clear, solitary ringing of the church-bell had a shrill and primitive sweetness to my ears. I cannot tell by what swift stages I entered into the faith and spirit of the place. No persuasion was used and, apparently, none was needed. My memory shows me almost at once treasuring small, gilt attendance cards, exchanging these for larger ones, quite at home in lesson-quarterlies, golden texts and the familiar hymn-tunes. The best of the latter had much to do with my conversion. They still seem to me, despite my present devotion to far other kinds of music, to express in no ignoble way, the triumphs and the aspirations of the Christian life. . . . The other night, with a dear companion, I passed a gaudy, modern church. A large congregation was singing Rock of Ages. As by a common impulse we stopped under the autumnal trees and listened. We knew, without speech, the strange *desiderium* in each other's hearts. For the poetry and beauty and the deep human need voiced by the Church came to us with that melody. Had we gone in, the banal prayers, the tawdry and vulgar sermon, the silly self-righteousness of the publicans and sinners within would have irritated or amused us . . . But in those distant years in St. Mark's the poetry and the beauty and the human need alone reached my mind and my emotions. I always staid after Sunday School to attend the morning service. But I am sure I hardly heard what the lank, gesticulating minister said. I accepted the Gospel story and the obvious implications of Pauline Christianity without question and felt—as I now know through critical retrospection—a spirit and a faith not wholly unlike that of the primitive Church. In the phraseology of our Protestant sects, I accepted Jesus as my personal Savior and cultivated, with vivid faith, the habit of prayer in which I persisted for many years.

My old life, however, was not dead. I read Homer and my German legends with the same imaginative naiveté as before. But I did absorb, unconsciously, of course, a very large set of moral and social conventions that are basic to the life of the average American. I stress the word absorb. There can be no question of reflection or conviction on the part of the child. But at the age of ten my emotional assimilation into the social group of which I was a physical member was complete. I would not have touched any alcoholic drink; I would have shrunk in horor from a divorced person; I would have felt a sense of moral discomfort in the presence of an avowed sceptic. I believed in the Blood of the Lamb . . . I find it hard not to let an ironic note slip into these phrases. But they mark the sober facts. If ever the child of immigrants embraced the faith of the folk among whom it came—I was that child. Insensibly almost I withdrew myself from my cousins and from the other Jewish children in the village. The sons and daughters of Mrs. C. were my chief playmates and, above all, a cousin of theirs who stirred my ever watchful sense of beauty. My parents I instinctively and unquestioningly exempted from this division. Nor did I talk about these things at home. I listened, as always, with deep pleasure to my mother's stories of her old home; I was interested in letters and gifts that came from our kinsmen across the ocean. But the old life grew fainter in its influence; it seemed hardly any more a part of this present experiencing. With the boys and girls of the Sunday School I went into the woods and fields for flowers at Easter, and when, at Christmas, my mother was saddened by yearning for her German home, I sorrowed only in her sorrow, myself quite at one with the life about me.

VI

I need scarcely say that my parents did not so readily adapt themselves to the folk-ways of the surprising land in which they found themselves. My mother especially, had an emotional tenacity which made her road the harder. Nor did she find a degree of compensation, as my father did, in the apparent absence of that pressure which he had experienced in a denser moral and economic environment. She consoled herself with the thought, however, that St. Mark's was but a rude backwoods village and steadily hoped for fairer conditions in some larger center of American civilization. It was from this point of view that she cultivated, in her scant leisure, a growing interest in English literature and worked hard at my training in the new language.

My father's case I have not stated adequately in the words—absence of pressure. For many weeks he was like one liberated from a dungeon. It was really recovery from mental illness. But he did not realize that and, in his impulsive way, attributed many extraordinary virtues to American life. He discussed politics with friends and neighbors—it was the Harrison-Cleveland campaign—read the old Eclectic Review, Byron and Dickens, played chess, and neglected his shop or treated the Negro customers with contempt-

uous disregard. His vision was fixed on far other
things. He was an excellent draughtsman and a store-
house of scientific knowledge. In Germany he had invented an intricate and clever machine, had obtained
patents for it there, in Austria and in France, and had
then sold it for a moderate sum. He now read in the
circular of a Washington firm of patent lawyers of the
urgent need for a non-refillable bottle. He accepted
this statement with the naiveté of a German and rigged
up a little work-room in the back of the shop. The
bottle was duly invented; the device was a notably in-
genious one. With a few tools he himself made several
beautifully finished models, drew up the specifications
and—considered his fortune made. For weeks we lived
in a state of exquisite anticipation. How much would
be offered? Twenty-five, fifty, a hundred thousand
dollars? My mother had her misgivings. But things
had gone so badly with the realities at hand that she
deliberately indulged in this beautiful dream ... It was
the last time ...

Must I add that the bubble burst? A letter came
from the patent attorneys so glaringly dishonest beneath all its speciousness that there was no room for
further self-deception. Certain brutal facts had to be
faced: trade had never been good and my father's
small capital was all but gone. For a good part of the
second summer we lived on rice and beans and such
tinned goods as were left on the shelves of the shop.
In autumn there was a respite of hope, but it was
quite brief. Creditors became troublesome and my
father, thoroughly German in this too, never dreamed
that he could leave them unpaid. He and my mother
sold their costly watches and chains and the remaining

stock in the shop brought a trifle at auction. When all debts had been paid there remained a little over four hundred dollars. With this sum my father determined to take his little family to Queenshaven, the nearest city of any size, and begin life anew. Throughout he was brave, cheerful and active. And to be sure he was only thirty-two years old and quite unable to estimate either the qualities of the environment to which he was going or the fatal development of certain forces within himself.

To me it was like starting out on a bright adventure. The days of the Southern winter were temperate and golden and a city seemed a fine place to go to. There would be the bay which I had seen and ships from all the ends of the earth. The thought of school I tried to put away from me. Then there was the fascinating bustle of packing and departure and a journey on the train which, though but four hours long, engaged my imagination. The days were full of life and promise to a boy of ten . . .

—A few years ago I passed through St. Mark's. The train rolled along the old embankment on the edge of which we used to gather wild blackberries. I am told that the village has grown and is now a county-seat. But it seemed small and remote. No doubt they are hustling and booming far more efficiently now and the smallness and remoteness were in my personal vision. But I know that in the early nineties of the last century there lingered in that village—as there did doubtless in many other places—something of that honest simplicity, that true democratic kindliness which we like to associate with the years of the primitive Republic. In the name of those qualities and the ideals which they illustrate the capitalistic tout still seeks to rob us, the brazen-tongued demagogue to betray us. Those things are gone. But as part of my imaginative inheritance as an American I own them by virtue of the two years of my childhood spent in St. Mark's in South Carolina.

CHAPTER III

The Making of an American

I

Queenshaven. I hear the sharp, quick rustling of the palmettos, the splash and murmur of the incoming tide, the melancholy song of Negroes across the bay; I see the iridescent plaster of the old walls at sunset, the crescent moon, so clear and silvery, over the light-house, the white magnolias in their olive foliage; I feel the full, rich sweetness of that incomparable air: above all, I can feel—across the gulfs of time and circumstance—the throb of the impassioned heart of my own youth . . . Stale phrases! I have tried before to describe the city. But I cannot do it. No man who has been young in the deep and true sense can render into words the scene of his youth. For that has taken its colors from a poetry, a passion, a tragic beauty that are beyond all speech. I see a sunset now and remark that it is fine and turn away to worry over yesterday's news from Russia and to-morrow's article. When I was a lad in Queenshaven the solemn, streaming sunsets over the bay were song and heroism and immortality to me. When the sun's great, red disc set behind the dusky islands and the first stars pulsed through the afterglow, I knew the universe to be divine and perfect and my eyes filled with tears. Wordsworth is right in the psychology of his great ode, whatever we may think of its metaphysics. Life encroaches upon our innermost selves and hardens and blunts them. The glory and the freshness are no more.

We arrived in Queenshaven on Washington's birthday. There was a parade which my mother took me to see, but the parade did not seem amusing to either of us and we went back to the house at which we were staying. It was a boarding-house recommended to us by Mrs. C. The house was a spacious one with a fine verandah on each story; around it extended a large though ill-kept garden. It was situated near the centre of the town; for two airy rooms and board for three my father payed eleven dollars a week. This was considered a very fair price in Queenshaven in 1892. The only thing we had to provide was the fuel for the two fire-places on chilly days. A supply of this we stored on the back verandah. And so, in a day or two, we were comfortably settled. Almost immediately, however, there came to us in some impalpable way a sense of something we had never felt in St. Mark's: invisible barriers seemed to arise about us, a silence seemed to fall where we were, an iron isolation to be established. All this was faint at first and could not be put into words; it took years to become a definite, tangible thing; I did not fully or consciously face it until it had been partly broken down. But that was too late. It had done its disastrous work.

Queenshaven was then—and I have reason to think it but little changed—a city of very rigid social groups. The majority of these were denominational in character: Catholic, Methodist, Baptist, Presbyterian. But

any family in any of these groups, primarily the
Protestant ones, that attained any degree of education or wealth, would tend to withdraw from its
original friends and social life and try, by any means,
to be reckoned among the small, conservative group
which consisted of the members and descendants of
the old Southern slave-holding aristocracy. For this
group was and is considered representative of the city
and has given to it all its flavor and romance and fame.
It was but a few years ago, for instance, that for the
first time a common man and not a member of a very
limited group of families was elected mayor of Queenshaven. Now it is clear that my parents could find no
friends among the humbler Catholics or Presbyterians
as such. And it is equally clear that persons who were
shedding their next of kin as one sheds old clothes in
a struggle to attain social distinction were not going to
impede their progress by so much as the acquaintance
of a little family of German Jews. The interesting
question arises: Why, then, did not my parents join
either one of two other groups—a German-American
and a Jewish one? Their instinct in this matter was
a fine although a quite tragically mistaken one. They
conceived the country in which they had made their
home as obviously one of English speech and culture.
Hence, without a shadow of disloyalty to their German
training, they desired to be at one with such of their
English-speaking countrymen as shared their tastes
in art and in literature and—*mutatis mutandis*—their
outlook on life. They saw no reason for associating
with North German peasants turned grocers (although
they had the kindliest feelings toward these sturdy and
excellent people), nor with rather ignorant, semi-

orthodox Jews from Posen. They had not done so in Berlin. Why should they in America where, as my father used to observe in those earliest years, a democratic spirit must prevail, and where neither poverty nor a humble employment could keep an educated man from the society of his intellectual equals. That was, according to him, the precise virtue of America, the fundamental spiritual implication of American life! The result of my parents' acceptance of this principle was utter friendlessness. They were left in a state of solitariness which would have broken stronger and better-balanced natures. The strain of wild eccentricity in my father's character sharpened, my mother's brooding melancholy deepened from year to year. When after nearly fifteen years in Queenshaven a breach was made in that inhuman wall, my father was hopelessly "queer" as a social being; my mother— whose sweet and gracious presence atoned with people for his rasping ways—had become morbid and morbidly suspicious of this belated kindness. I look back and see with a cruel clearness how that loneliness ate into their hearts; how though they rarely spoke of it, they were warped and embittered by it. The same dreary tasks day after day, year after year; the same lonely lamplight in the evening; never a knock at the door or the sound of a friendly voice. And for the first ten years they were too poor to go to the theatre or to concerts.

After various other attempts my father drifted into the furniture business. He was employed by a large house to sell furniture among the Negroes and collect the installments from week to week. After a day of this wretched toil—which he did well and for

which, during the second decade, he was not ill-paid—
I have seen him spend the evening intensely absorbed
in Bradley's Appearance and Reality. Such was his
real life. And my mother was, in her native tongue,
a true poet. And never a footstep on the stair ... They
had accepted the promise of American life. Nor, be
it observed, would their fate have been different in a
larger and more typical American community. Happier
it would have been, no doubt. For they would have
fallen in with cultivated Germans and Jews. But that,
clearly, does not touch the problem. It was in Queenshaven that the Anglo-American ideal of assimilation
which they embraced could be tested and adjudged.

II

The situation, as I have said, took some years to
define itself. Immediately there was, for us all, the
beauty and stir of the town. For me, above all, there
was that house with its verandahs and its tangled garden. The early Southern spring came upon the city
almost at once, first with lilies and the innumerable
blossoms of the wistaria, then with roses that, dotting
a gnarled, old vine, trembled at our very windows and
filled the verandah with petals. My mother and I took
daily walks and inhaled the fragrant loveliness of the
place and the season. But I was always glad to return to the house. I played at its being a castle and
myself, upon the verandah, a warder, a Scottish archer
at some dark keep in France. For at an auction house
my father had bought a very good set of the Waverly
novels and I was living in a magnificent world, a pageant of infinite variety and splendor. The tall, green

double-columned volumes were rarely out of my hands.
Within a few months I had read all the novels, or
nearly all. I never succeeded in finishing Count Robert of Paris, although it has left with me a vision of
empty Byzantine halls through which is heard the ringing echo of a solitary mailed tread; I did not read
Waverly till years later. My favorites which were soon
definitely chosen I read tirelessly over and over:
Quentin Durward, The Talisman, The Heart of Mid-
lothian, Rob Roy, The Betrothed, The Black Dwarf,
Anne of Geierstein, A Legend of Montrose. I liked the
gloomy and the romantic; that is clear. But character
was beginning to appeal to me too, and I tasted to the
full of the fine essential humanity of the Dean family,
of the Baillie Nicol Jarvie, of the redoubtable Dugald
Dalgetty. I worshipped Diana Vernon in all my waking dreams. My students in later years told me they
cannot read Scott. Strange. They were not commonly so sensitive to a lack of grace and finish in style and
structure. And what a creator of men and scenes and
actions Sir Walter was! What sweep he had, what
imagination, what ample power. As for me, I enjoyed
even those opening chapters of which I hear such
querulous complaints; I enjoyed the very notes and
puzzled out the crabbed Latin as soon as I could and
felt the pride of knowledge. I was glad many of the
novels were long. They seemed like the weeks and
months of childhood; one could really live in them and
forget the troublesome world of duties and compul-
sions.

A few months later came another of those massive
revelations which are among the glories of our earlier
years: Dickens. In lank, acrid-smelling, paper-backed

volumes came Pickwick, Nickleby, Chuzzlewit, Oliver
Twist, A Tale of Two Cities. Not, alas, David Copper-
field. The false, strained effort in A Tale of Two
Cities I was too young to perceive. Yet I know that I
could not live in it as richly and as fully as in the
others—books which again contained a world. Not a
world, I think now, that has much veracity or permanent significance, but in its vast and busy imaginative
structure self-consistent, racy, and full of fine, concrete
things—beef and punch and stage-coaches and gaols,
thwackings and counting-houses, practical jokes and
prisons, mud and rags and laughter . . .

I still prayed every night. But these books absorbed me and I went neither to Sunday School nor to
church. My faith was tenacious enough, but it grew
less active. Then, by the merest accident, there came
a brief but burning revelation. The boarding-house
was kept by an Irish family, friendly and far from
ignorant. The head of the house, a small, straight,
white-bearded, crimson-faced man, very silent and always more or less in liquor, took a fancy to me. One
Sunday morning we began to talk. He had been a sea-
faring man in his youth and I found his talk sharp
with the tang of ships and voyages. I fetched my hat
and walked on with him. Somehow, presently, I found
myself beside him in the family pew in the old pro-
Cathedral and witnessed the celebration of a High
Mass.

The reading of Scott had not left me without an
imaginative perception of the rich historic dignity, the
human associations of the Roman ritual. But it touched
to the very quick my sense of beauty. I was powerless before it as I am before beauty still. The organ

was the best I had ever heard and my taste in music was even then not uncultivated. But the glimmering vestments of the priests, the dreamy candles, the strange bell, the elevation of the Host on which fell a pencil of softened light—all these things moved me profoundly. And I still think that, if one could but grant the tremendous premises all these symbols do, in a lovely and human fashion, elevate and attune the soul . . . When we came out of the dusky church the sunlight seemed raw and like an affront. I went home but did not speak of what I had experienced. All week long, however, the altar candles shone like fiery topazes in my waking dreams and the sonorous music echoed in my ears. I was sorry that I had not a rosary as a visible symbol of that marvelous church.

I went to mass every Sunday. A Catholic family of French descent moved into the boarding-house; the children and I became friends and so I was naturally drawn to go with them. The services became my great passion. I even went to Vespers, and more and more it seemed to me that to be a priest of this Church would be a calling that would satisfy every instinct of my nature. Such was the first plan that I made for my adult years . . .

Was it all a child's shallow religiosity? Not all, I think. For I had a sense, shadowy and inarticulate, but deep enough, of our homelessness in the universe, of our terrible helplessness before it. I had seen something of misfortune and uncertainty and change and my mind desired then as, with such frugal hope, it does now, a point of permanence in the "vast driftings of the cosmic weather," a power in which there is no variableness, neither shadow of turning.

[63]

And I had a dream which added another element to my inner life, a dream that has stayed with me in its stark and preternatural vividness these many years. I dreamed that I was in a large, empty room with brown walls. The door opened slowly and as it opened my heart beat with insupportable fear. My mother entered and I saw at once that her face was ghastly white. She did not speak. She looked into my eyes and fell forward, and I heard the thud of her head on the wood . . . From that time on my prayers were all propitiatory. I often prayed and wept in an agony of apprehension. I would stop on the street suddenly and pray to ward off evil from her. I invented strange, childish rituals in the efficacy of which I would trust for a time and then abandon them for others. My freedom from care was gone beyond recall and all my religious emotions centered about an inner core of gloom.

III

In October, 1893, after an oral examination which, thanks to my mother's instruction, I passed with ease, I was admitted to the High School of Queenshaven. The school building is plain and dignified, somewhat after the fashion of an English mansion of the eighteenth century. What the school has become in recent years I do not know. I have heard rumors of courses in bookkeeping and shorthand and other dexterities that have nothing to do with the education of youth. In my time it was a good school. The pupils were all boys and they were taught by men. They were young enough to be grounded in the necessities of a liberal education without having their callow judgment consulted, and to be caned when they were lazy or rowdy. The school had one grave fault: Greek was an elective study. Through this fault my life sustained an irreparable loss. Yet when I consider what might have happened to my mind if the school had been like the High Schools of 1921, I am filled with a sense of gratitude. For I was enabled to lay the foundations of a sound and permanent knowledge of Latin and French; I was taught to study with thoroughness and accuracy under pain of tangible and very wholesome penalties, and it was not the fault of the school that my mind was and is all but impervious to any form of mathematical reasoning.

I passed into the rough and tumble of school life with a distinct shudder. There was no direct hazing but there was a good deal of rather cruel horse-play. You were apt to be tripped up and thrown on your back, to have pins and needles stuck viciously into you, to be held under the pump until you nearly choked. Also, during the first year, I was taunted with being a foreigner and a Jew. One boy especially tormented me—a tallish fellow with huge mouth always distorted by idiotic laughter, hateful, offstanding ears and small, greenish eyes. I was no match for him in strength and he persisted in cuffing and thumping and taunting me. I tried to avoid him, for I shrank from the thought of touching him as shudderingly as I did from his touch. Then, one day he clapped me brutally on the back and yelled with laughter. Two scarlet lights danced before my eyes and I leapt at his throat. Boys hurried from all sides of the play-ground and formed a ring around us. Cries arose: "Fight fair!" I remembered how the contemptuous thoughts raced through my brain. Fight fair! Oh yes, give the overgrown lout a chance to trounce me as a reward for months of bruises and insults. I didn't want to fight him and suffer more undeserved pain and humiliation. I wanted to hurt him, to hurt him so effectively that he would never again dare lay his red, bony claws on me. I did. A teacher had to come into the yard and order me to be torn from my gasping and bloody victim. I had no trouble after that . . .

Gradually, too, I fell in with a group of boys that belonged to the gentler families of Queenshaven. I shall have more to say of them later, for these classmates passed together through school and college with me and so lived on terms of daily intimacy with me for eight years. Through their companionship, at all events, I soon felt at home in the school, an equal among equals in play and study.

I have said that our teachers were men. Real men, I hasten to add, not the spiritual starvelings who are content nowadays with the wage-slavery of the High School. The salaries of these Queenshaven teachers were rather better than such salaries are to-day and the purchasing power of money was of course far greater. The principal was the only man I have ever known who truly embodied the peculiar ideal of the Christian gentleman. He had both sweetness and strength, profound piety and wide charity. I can still see the beautiful benevolence in his searching blue eyes and hear his clear, bell-like voice. I do not know whether he consciously thought of the methods of Arnold of Rugby; it is certain that he practiced them. The better natured of my schoolmates and I never resented his punishments; we knew he was incapable of inflicting them until in his kind and manly judgment forgiveness would have been morally harmful to the offender. His influence and example drew me back to the Methodist church ... It is a sad reflection that this good man's end was pitiful. A trusted brother in the church absconded with all our principal's modest savings. They were small enough, for he was liberal in his charities beyond the bounds of discretion. But this blow both in its moral and in its physical aspect overwhelmed him. He fell into a state of melancholia and I remember him, in later years, a mild, vague-eyed, broken figure on the Queenshaven streets.

I shall not linger over the burly and severe but sound pedagogue who taught us history and physics nor over the graceful youth—still young and vivid in his middle age—who taught French and German with a stringent accuracy and sternness that added virility to his Greek profile and his curving locks. It is on our teacher of Latin that I must dwell. I cannot estimate his influence over me. To this day I find myself using locutions and mannerisms that are ultimately traceable to him. He was—I beg his pardon for writing of him as in the past, but to me he lives only in the past, though admirably and fruitfully to others in their present—he was the son of an Italian gentleman, obviously of gentle lineage and exquisite breeding. His face and head and hands and form had in them something indescribably Roman. Roman of the empire. But for his severer modern morals he might have been a friend of Petronius and, like him, an *arbiter elegantiarum.* Or, from another point of view, a gentleman of the age of Queen Ann—a friend of Addison. Of course this does not render the whole man. But he was singularly free from all the modern maladies of the soul—a devout Catholic with a frugal and pagan delight in the good things of the world, a lover of the arts without morbid intensity or perverting ambitions, a believer in that golden mean which he interpreted so well. I need hardly say that the particular objects of his tireless and exquisite zeal were Vergil and Horace and, among English writers, Milton and Tennyson and Thackeray.

As a teacher he was strict, though always with a light touch—stinging the lazy and loutish by some ironic turn of speech. He taught us to appreciate a fine and mellow Latinity as well as the human warmth and living power of the literature we read. But he was tireless, too, in the humbler portions of his task. I find that I know my Latin accidence and syntax better to-day than graduate students who "major" in Latin at our universities. And I can still hear his voice as, repeating some line of Vergil, he first awakened me to the magic of a great and perfect style.

> " . . . et jam nox umida coelo
> praecipitat suadentque cadentia sidera somnos."

It was in the third year of High School. He was teaching us to scan Vergil. We were repeating a passage in unison. Suddenly he swung on his heel and pointed his finger straight at me: "That is the only boy who has a natural ear for verse!" he cried. A keen, strange quiver went through me. I realized the meaning suddenly of that constant scribbling which I had been impelled to during the preceding months. I had a gift for literature! I knew it now; I never doubted it again. My fate had found me.

IV

I continued to buy little note-books and to fill
them with verse. I neglected my tasks at school and
bore my punishments stolidly. When my father explained problems in mathematics or physics to me, I
did not listen and took his solutions to school. They
were correct, of course, but I could not explain them.
I wrote dozens of stanzas a day; I was obsessed by a
strange, aching fever and found no relief but in verse.
The verse, of course, was childish—half sentimental,
half-religious—yet often full of a bitter and, as it now
seems to me, pathetic yearning. I can see myself—
(we had long moved into the two upper floors of a
pleasant enough house)—a boy of thirteen, on the up-
stairs verandah that faced the sunset, watching the
trees grow dark against the sky and the evening star
emerge. There I stood or sat throbbing with a passion
for poetry that I still think was rare and not ignoble.
No, for there was blended with it a profound humility,
an earnest realization of the utter worthlessness of
what I was writing and would write for years to come.
Only at the end of that long vista of years shone the
star of my hope. Some day, somehow, I would be
a poet.

I abandoned the German books of my childhood. I
stopped speaking German even at home. Seeking relief from the passion and the yearning that consumed
me I read, half-surreptitiously, the African tales of
Rider Haggard or even cheap detective stories. But
this period of merely silly reading was brief. By a
happy chance I became acquainted with a writer who
gave tone and vigor to my boyish mind and fixed it

upon great ideas and great affairs. I am, of course, aware now of everything that can be said against Macaulay. But even now I can look with kindness upon his swaggering omniscience, his two-penny optimism, his unscrupulous rhetoric. He led me when I was half a child to Milton and Dryden and Johnson. But for his noble love of letters I might have been like those contemporary youngsters who find Paradise Lost dull and The Hind and the Panther stupid and The Lives of The Poets old-fashioned. And he gave scope to my imagination in the world of man and history and with him I shared the pageantry of Clive's conquests and was stirred by the trial of Hastings and followed the campaigns of the great Frederic. My acquaintance with him began curiously. Our principal had sent me on an errand to another class-room. There the teacher was reading to the boys a description of the black hole at Calcutta. The impression of that passage stayed with me for many days. Finally I asked a boy in that class the name of the author and went home and forthwith demanded that author's works. So on my thirteenth birthday, which was but a few weeks distant, my parents gave me a plain three-volume edition of the Essays. I was intensely happy. I needed nothing more that whole summer. I read the essays over and over again—the Addison, the Johnson, the Leigh Hunt—and determined to become not only a poet but a scholar and a man of letters.

For a whole year the reading of Macaulay was my chief pleasure. I read novels, at times, of course. For in my boyhood, as now, I always combined desultory with intensive reading. And my passion for writing verse increased rather than diminished. But the greatest revelation of my boyhood, the revelation that awakened me definitely to literature as a fine art, came during the last year of my High School course. For during that year we read under our admirable teacher the Odes of Horace.

What first enchanted me was the poet's metrical systems, the nervous, sonorous Alcaic, the restrained pathos of the Sapphic cadences, the surge-like sweep and recoil of the great Archilochian measures. Was ever language wrought into a larger music? There were lines and fragments that I repeated over and over to myself with endless rapture:

"Cras ingens iterabimus aequor,"

and

". . . sors exitura et nos in aeternum
exsilium impositura cymbae."

And that other which, years later, I found had also evoked the wonder and delight of Stevenson:

"aut Lacedaemonium Tarentum."

I cared for the poet's matter too: his mellowness, his essential highmindedness, the sad serenity of his acceptance of life, his sober wisdom, the playfulness that is never very far from a characteristic Latin sense of the transitoriness of all things. But what influenced me most deeply was his stylistic finish and I absorbed into my innermost being a hundred just and terse and lovely phrases that I shall remember as long as I remember anything. I looked at my own verses and their flabby fatuousness made my cheeks burn. I swore not to write again until I had learned

to write, and set about learning by translating the
odes of Horace. I knew but dimly that a host of mature and learned writers had tried their skill upon
my poet. I was acquainted with Milton's rendering of
the "Quis multa gracilis," which, with all proper
reverence, I did not think wonderful. So I hammered
away, quite guilelessly at my own versions. One of
them—it was of the radiant and yet melancholy "Dif-
fugere nives" (IV, 7.)—seemed to me not so bad. I
put the manuscript in my pocket. But every day when
I heard the keen voice of our teacher my courage
failed me. At the end of weeks filled with trepidation
and misery I handed him the folded sheet. We took
our seats. He spread out the paper before him on the
desk. I heard my heart beat and the blood buzz and
hum in my ears. His face grew very red as it did
when he was angry and my heart nearly stopped. He
looked up and gave me one of his vivid glances. "Did
you do that yourself?" I could only nod. But evidently he saw the desperate sincerity in my eyes. He
sprang up and smiled, and his smiles were very brilliant. "It needs improvement here and there," he
said. "But it's good, it's charming! You will go far
—far!" And he read it to the class.

I suppose we grow stolid as we grow older. Doubtless, too, I was more sensitively attuned than most
boys of fourteen. But the hours and days that followed this incident were such as to outweigh a good
many of the sorrows and hungers of life. I took the
story home to my father and mother and they were
moved by it. For in their starved and lonely lives
they had set all their hopes on me. And these hopes
were liberal and fine. From that day on they shared

my ambition that I was to be a scholar and a man of letters, even though that meant a renunciation of the world's material prizes and rewards.

V

During my last year at High School, however, a difficulty beset me which during hours and days made life seem hideous and hopeless. There arose, very sharply and imperiously, the consciousness of sex. By a degrading and stupid convention the problem of sex is regarded as non-existent among Anglo-Americans. No doubt, men tell jokes. . . . So did the boys with whom I went to school—pointless, nasty jokes. But these boys, like many of my friends later, would have regarded a discussion of sex, the immense central problem of sex, as a little vulgar and more than a little disconcerting. And my Americanization was complete. I shared that point of view or, at least, very potently believed that I shared it. No power on earth could have dragged from me a hint of my emotions. I attended a Methodist church. I was a member of the Epworth league. Naturally I soon fell into a wretched conviction of sin and tried to double the zeal of my religious exercises. Yet all my inner life was like a clear pool that had been muddied and defiled. Neither prayer nor study were of much avail at certain hours. Relentlessly my mind drifted off into imaginings that filled me with terror, but that seem to me now, as I recall them, not only harmless but rather poetical. I was the more convinced of the wickedness of my thoughts by the absurd exaltation of woman which is so characteristic a note of Southern

life. I had been taught by my whole social environment
to believe that woman is a being without passion, without any feelings of the grosser sort. No one who has
not lived in the South will credit the universality and
blatancy of this preposterous folly. It imparts to the
Southern gentleman a courtesy to "good" women
which no self-sustaining human being needs; it makes
his behavior to women who are not "good" literally
currish. But these conventions had entered into the
very texture of my life. Nothing could have persuaded
me that I would ever have thoughts as "ungentle-
manly" as those I have just set down. A gentleman
believed that the South was in the right in the War
between the States, that Christianity was the true religion—(to be merely suspected of liberality in points
of doctrine added a bold, mysterious charm provided
you were a man and over fifty)—that the Democratic
party was the only means, under Providence, of saving
the White Race from obliteration by the Nigger, that
good women are sexless—"sweet and pure" was the
formula—and that in a harlot's house you must keep
on your hat. And we were trained to be "young gentlemen." Well, the good people succeeded with me.
I shared their faith and their morals and my boyish
soul was tormented and warped. . . . Some years later
with a crowd of college-boys—all pretty drunk—I went
into a harlot's house. We came out as we had gone in.
I had wanted hard to take my hat off. The insult
seemed so futile and so cruel. But I didn't dare risk
the gibes of my comrades. I was a young gentleman.

In one respect only did I fail to achieve a complete
conformity. It was in the matter of games. This circumstance added, of course, to the distress of my de-

VI

It is clear then that, at the age of fifteen, I was an American, a Southerner and a Christian. My home, it may be urged, was foreign in spirit. But that was true to a very much slighter extent than may be supposed. For my father and mother were both bookish people and all the books they read were English. Our conversation, whether it turned upon these books, as it often did, or upon my father's business or my studies was all of the very texture of the civilization amid which we lived. My mother with that self-distrust which was always hers, spoke less and less of the memories which formed so large a part of her inner life. In a superficial sense I shared her joy, to be sure, in letters and gifts from Germany. Or, at least, I was happy in her happiness. For I was intensely sensitive to her needs and moods. My Americanization was, nevertheless, complete. It differed, to be quite scrupulous, from the Americanism of my comrades at school and college, but it differed by a touch of self-consciousness and a touch of militancy. It was at this time that, in my thoughts and emotions, I came upon a distinct and involuntary hostility to everything either Jewish or German. I seemed to have a premonition that, in some subtle way, these elements in my life and fate might come between me and the one thing in the world I cared for supremely—the poetry of the English tongue.

I recall a certain Christmas. My father's employer had given him a present in money. And we three went out into the Queenshaven streets. They were ill-lit and there was no moon. But I remember the clear sparkle

of the large stars over the small, dark houses. A chill
wind blew in from the bay, but the streets were dry
and clean. I cannot recall what my father bought for
my mother or for himself. But I asked for a copy of
Tennyson. And I took home with me the Globe edition.

I needed nothing more; my mind and my heart
were filled. Yet I did not read many poems to the
end. For their beauty overwhelmed me and a lump
came into my throat and my eyes blurred. Not at the
story or the sentiments to which, indeed, I scarcely
attended. But at the sheer beauty of the diction and
the versification. The May Queen and The Grandmother left me cold. I was rather ashamed for Tennyson that he had written them. The poems that gave
me such unbearable keenness of delight were The
Dying Swan, The Lotos Eaters, the Lines to Vergil!
. . . Soon thereafter, deliberately teaching myself to
read French for pleasure, I read for the first time
Taine's Histoire de la littérature anglaise and was
overcome with indignation and disgust at the famous
parallel between Tennyson and Musset. I borrowed
the Frenchman's verses which I understood but ill.
Well enough, however, it seemed to me, to think his
work almost vulgar and quite trivial compared to the
aristocratic sweetness, the noble attitude of England's
laureate. Could spiritual Americanization in a lad
have gone farther? Could anyone native-born have
held sentiments more correct with a higher passion? . . .

I buried the rebellious things in me deeper and
deeper—sex and doubt. I hated to admit the fact of
our social isolation. Not out of snobbishness. But
because I wished to live in harmony with the society
of which, by virtue of its English speech and ideals, I

felt myself so integral a part. So I deliberately shut my eyes to that exclusion which, of course, I felt far less keenly than my parents. I saw something of my comrades, I had my poetry; I took long daily walks with my mother, walks which I loved. For her sensitive sympathy never failed. My father did not care for verse as verse; my schoolfellows respected my ability without comprehending my tastes. She was my confidant and friend.

I spent the summer vacation that followed my graduation from High School in turning out more versions of Horace, in writing verses of my own and in enormous reading. I looked forward to autumn and to my entering college with subdued but keen happiness. I meant to make a name for myself at the famous old college and I also knew now the means by which I was to conquer for myself a life of learned ease and poetical activity, and for my parents a secure and pleasant future. I meant to be—consider the immense irony of these boyish hopes and assurances—a professor of English literature.

CHAPTER IV

The Making of an Anglo-American

I

The campus of the College of Queenshaven occupies several city blocks. Tall trees stand in it and the shadows of their branches tremble in the sunshine upon the Grecian portico and on the warm, brown walls of the old building. A place of peace—gentle with an eighteenth century repose. There are not students enough for boisterousness, no bleak or snowy weather ever adds a touch of roughness or hardship to the scene. No engineering courses had been established in my time; the chair of biology was practically vacant. We strolled across the campus learning to smoke cigarettes or pipes, reading our Latin or our English poets. Chemistry and mathematics were the snakes in my Paradise. I could not crush them, but I tried to forget their existence except during the actual hours of recitation and laboratory practice. The latter were hideous. Outside the leaves fluttered and the swallows wheeled and poetry sounded with her golden voice. And I had to potter around with noxious and stenchful stuffs. Of the cosmic meaning of these experiments no one told me a word. What I have learned of the problem of matter as it affects our thinking concerning man and God I have learned for myself. I hated having to remember how you manufacture sulphuric acid or get zinc from its ore. But these troubles were small and transitory. If I had not been so long a pedagogue by trade, fiercely resentful of the time an unilluminating science-teaching steals from the humanities, these scars upon the memories of my college life would be forgotten. For that life was, upon the whole, happy and the sinister elements grew to be so only through their consequences.

My freshman year was marked by several radical and fortunate changes in the college. A new president was called: an energetic young man, a scholar and a thinker; my admirable old teacher of Latin was transferred from the high school to our college; a young man was brought from a Western university to fill the chair of English. The last event was the most important of all to me. For years Ferris was the dominant influence in my life. He more than any one made me what I was during my early manhood. I bore him a true affection; I bear him that affection still. Deep, strange, silent things seemed to divide us for a time. But that division is over. We are to-day upon a firmer ground of friendship and understanding than ever before. Ferris was under thirty when he came to Queenshaven, but already his hair was completely white. His mouth was hidden under a drooping blond mustache; his prominent features were his sensitive nose, his high, fine, narrow forehead, his large violet-blue eyes. A fragile, gracious, spiritually virile figure—a trifle slovenly, unkempt, with an absorbed, aloof air that would yield to a very human, quaintly sweet smile. He was very shy and had a touch of irony in his speech. The average student didn't like him; to the exceptional student he came at once to mean much. To me—everything. I had had practically no instruction in English and Ferris took notice of me at once, of my ambition and of my talent. He taught me how to train myself to write; he gave me generously of his time; he paid my efforts the fine tribute of searching criticism and merciless veracity. During the four years that I was his pupil I do not think he praised me twice. But now and then a certain earnestness, almost solemnity would come into his eyes and then I knew that I had approached my goal a little nearer. For I recognized in him at once a singularly subtle and exquisitely tempered literary intelligence. Delicate in health, drifting through the years down the warm, enervating current of Queenshaven life, he has done nothing. I suppose he still sits by the library window or in his study, playing with a reed-stemmed clay-pipe, savoring with that wonderful aesthetic taste of his the finest literature, planning a little and sinking back into his delicate Epicureanism. A stronger body, a rougher life, a goad of love or hunger, a little less consciousness of gentility—and he might have been a master.

Gentility! He could not even in those years quite forget that his father, a professor at Washington college, had been a friend and colleague of General Lee and that he was a Virginian aristocrat. His mind had fared forth boldly on all the quests of man; apparently his intellectual flexibility and moral freedom were boundless. But at the slightest translation of that freedom into action, were it by so much as a vivid gesture, a spiritual discomfort seized him and the gentleman conquered the man. Since art means passion and since all passion has a touch of wildness, he was ever too much of a gentleman to be an artist. Not with his mind and heart, but with his unconquerable tribal self he always loved something else—a quiet manner, reserve of speech, an aristocratic nose—a little better than he loved truth or beauty. To illustrate the right humility before greatness he once told his students that he would have been glad to blacken Shakespeare's boots. He was quite sincere, but he would not have stood the test. The real Shakespeare—the morbid lover, the truant husband, the shabby actor, the poet whose divine energy of speech must have lent storm and flame to his daily discourse—that man would have filled Ferris with discomfort and dismay. . . . We saw a very great deal of each other in the course of the years and I know that his affection for me was very real. But he never, I think, quite forgave me for being what I am.

My mother, with a woman's sensitiveness, had a perception, unreasonable but very real, of the ultimate truth. At home I spoke of Ferris daily during my four years at college. He and his influence filled my life. And often my mother would hint at a touch of disloyalty in him to me. I always defended him hotly, and indeed her reasons were invariably quite wrong. But the sting of the situation was that I knew her to be in the right. In the best and deepest hours we spent together there was in him a shadow of withdrawal from me—a shadow of watchfulness, of guardedness. . . . A shadow, but it was there. He too must have realized it, must have reflected on it, for I also stood for something in his life, and I am unwilling to believe that such a nature as his yielded without a struggle to the injustice of its tribal self. That shadow, at all events, is gone now and it seems hateful to record it. But I must do so since during many years it remained in my mind as the symbol of an essential isolation.

II

Such feelings and reflections, of course, occupied my mind but at occasional, comfortless moments during my years at college. Had I been but a shade less sensitive, even these moments would have been spared me. My true life was given over to the absorption of Ferris' teaching, of his intimate, unspoken, but ever richly implied point of view. That point of view I can sum up in but one word, and that word is—England. His attitude to the intellectual and artistic life of America was a little detached, a little patronizing, a little amused. The serious thing in American life to him was its continuing of those English social traditions within our older commonwealths of which he was the product. But the home of his soul and of his imagination was by some Surrey lane or Kentish field or Westmoreland lake. To me, whose love of English poetry had been so largely an aesthetic rapture, he communicated those other and even richer associations which soon blended in my inner life, as they had done in his, into a spiritual loyalty to England that was all the deeper because we were forbidden the more obvious loyalties granted to her children and her citizens. We were glad and proud to be the dependents and colonials of that mighty mother from whom came the song and the beauty, the traditions and the fair imaginings that were the best of life to us. . . . Ferris knew both French and German well. But he read those foreign literatures with a cool and somewhat arrogant curiosity. And, during my boyish years, I absorbed that attitude as well.

England! How should I not have loved her? I knew nothing of life. And there were

> The magic casements opening on the foam
> Of perilous seas in fairy lands forlorn—

there that road to Canterbury along which the immortal pilgrims fared; there were the gardens and the learned seats where Milton studied and Gray brooded and Tennyson wove those early all too golden verses; there was that other, lovelier city of the dreamy spires where Newman's voice floated through Saint Mary's chapel and the lad Arnold heard it and remembered it forever. There was that motley city of the thousand visions: Milton in blindness beholding the bowers of Paradise; Dryden at Will's coffee-house and Pope, a large-eyed, crooked child seeing the great, old man; Addison writing The Campaign in shabby lodgings; Johnson talking out of the depth of his noble, sombre heart; the fiery Hazlitt, the exquisite Lamb gathered about Coleridge in deep, heroic talk, and Shelley, wild-eyed, weaving here too the colors of his incomparable dreams. And far beyond the city were Windermere, clothed so truly to me in

> A light that never was on sea or land
> The consecration and the poet's dream,

and, most sacred of all and most beloved—Laleham churchyard where Arnold sleeps. How faint these

fragments of that imaginative vision of England! I
summon it before me again as it arose in my soul in
those impressionable years in all its storied wealth,
in all its singing splendor. No bodily eye was needed.
I knew the whiteness of the Dover cliffs, the "league-
long rollers" on the Isle of Wight, the sylvan Wye
"that wanderer through the woods," and that

> wet, bird-haunted, English lawn

the thought of which came with a pang of beauty which
was almost pain. What wonder that in my mind, taking color from my friend's, this England, this land of
the soul, became indissolubly one with that British
empire which we conceived of as spreading the noble
things we loved to the ends of the earth. We rejoiced,
like the very children of her soil, in her "far-flung
battle line," and like the poet she drove out and killed,
heard with our very ears and with our very hearts

> The measured roll of English drums
> Beat at the gates of Kandahar.

In 1898 or 1899 I read an article on Kipling in the
Quarterly Review. I took his books from the library
and was at once drawn into the full current of British
imperialism. Of his verses, though I admired and imi-
tated them, I always had a lurking, unadmitted doubt.
But the stories took me by storm. And the best of
them are, indeed, beyond praise in their magnificent
concreteness, their Homeric freshness. The shallow-
ness and meanness of the man's outlook on life were
quite beyond my perception. I let what is surely the
enduring part of him persuade me to accept not only
the artist but also the politician. I heartily believed

a Little Englander to be a fool and a contemptible fool; I conceived of the Boers not as obstacles to conquest and rapacity but to the spreading of a heaven-sent light. I believed that America was, by virtue of our community of speech and literature with England, a sharer in this light which was to be forcibly shed upon all the dark places of the earth, and I found it hard to forgive William Vaughan Moody for counselling us in his great Ode Written In A Time Of Hesitation to let the island men of the Philippines go free. . . . I found the other day, among old papers, a manuscript ode to England which I wrote when I was eighteen. I remember that Ferris praised it and, indeed, the verses are not without merit. But it interested me as confirming so thoroughly the facts in my development which I have here set down. I was a Pan-Angle of the purest type; so was Ferris, so were my classmates—lads of English and Anglicized French Huguenot descent—so were the half dozen cultivated lawyers and business men and journalists in the community who, about this time, began to take an interest in me and in my work. All, at least, except one. But he, a wealthy Jewish physician who had turned Methodist in his boyhood, avoided all questionable subjects, prayed at love feasts in church and, though he surreptitiously distributed alms among the poor Jews of the city, achieved a complete conformity of demeanor. My father, furthermore, became as fervid an admirer of Kipling as myself. The poet's politics he scarcely noted, for he had not my inner reasons for a blind adherence to that faith. He did not want to be an English poet. . . . Acquaintances, with a warning gravity of demeanor, whispered to me later that I haven't a sense of what England stands for in the world. Who was ever firmer in that faith? Not Eliot nor Hibben nor a wilderness of blood-thirsty professors. Only I've done a little living, a little thinking . . . especially a little thinking since. That grave look in my friends' eyes which used to impress me seems like the blank gravity of idiot children. . . .

III

I still, during these years, attended the Methodist church, taught Sunday School and was a leader in the Epworth League. I did this partly because, up to my junior year, my Christian faith, though cooler, was still unshaken, partly through the influence and friendship of the physician whom I have mentioned, but also because I found a good deal of unreserved human friendliness among these people. And I needed this. The relations between my class-mates and myself were very cordial; several of them often visited me as I did them. Yet there always came a point at which I felt excluded. They themselves belonged to a definite social group. They neither drew me into this group nor did they have the good sense or good feeling to be silent before me concerning these more intimate affairs. I do not think their exclusion of me was at all a matter of reason or determination; it was quite instinctive. By virtue of my work on the college magazine and the attitude of the professors toward me, they respected me. Personally they liked me well enough and elected me, without hesitation, in due time, president of our literary society and editor-in-chief of the magazine. As tribesmen their resistance to me

was tacit but final. A pushing or insinuating fellow
might, assuredly, have made his way. But my sensitiveness was so alert that I, no doubt, at times created
division by suspecting it and at once shrinking away.
But of the fundamental fact there could be no doubt.
It was terribly confirmed to me by an incident in my
senior year. I was the most prominent student on the
campus. My classmates called themselves my friends
—voluntarily and without my seeking. And these very
friends gathered to form the first chapter of a Greek
letter fraternity at our college and—left me out. I did
not know then that the fraternities do not admit Jews.
I do not know now whether they practice this exclusion
tacitly or by regulation. I never spoke of the incident
either at school or at home. Our president who
founded the chapter does not know to this day that I
so much as observed the matter. I did, with a profound discouragement, with a momentary grim pre-
vision of the future which I fought bitterly to blot
out lest I should lose all my hopes and see all my life
crumble before me at eighteen. I withdrew into myself with sullen pride and intensified ambition, convinced that the incident was local, exceptional, unrep-
resentative and un-American. Such was my simple
faith. . . .

Gradually, too, I was losing the satisfaction that
I had once taken in the society of my Methodist friends.
For in my eighteenth year the world began to clear
for me. Until then my passion for literature had been
so exclusive that neither my reasoning power nor my
power of observation had developed. These were now
somewhat suddenly awakened and were the source of
constant, sharp revelations. I remember a garden

party given by a bishop's widow to the young people
of the Epworth League. It was a very charming garden with beds full of old-fashioned flowers; honey-
suckle and clematis covered the piazza that gave on
the lawn. There were chairs and tables and ice-cream
and cakes were served by girls dressed in white. The
glint of the sunlight on their smooth hair and the rustle of their starched skirts gave me a faint, sensuous
pleasure. And one of the girls had a slow, liquid
laugh. The young men, in duck trousers and blue
coats, were clerks, with a sprinkling of students from
a Methodist college. For almost the first time I listened to the talk objectively—the kind of talk carried
on a thousand times a day in a thousand American
communities. It was mostly what is known as chaff,
feeble to the point of imbecility. How could these
people laugh at it? Laugh they did. But the laughter
though loud was without true mirth. For that requires
a vigor either of mind or temper that was far to seek.
It was all witless, stale and puerile beyond conception
—refined through sheer weakness, well-mannered and
yet incurably ill-bred. The pastor went from table
to table—a tall, bony, large-mouthed man. He spoke
of the beauty of the afternoon and of the delightfulness
of seeing young people so happy. His long, pale lips
writhed in smiles over his jagged teeth. As he pressed
my hand all I could think of was his fondness for
talking about purity, and of his wife, emaciated with
child-bearing, and their six or seven small, depressed
children. . . . A withered, eager, bead-eyed spinster
told of a friend of hers who was a missionary in Mexico. I wondered if the Mexicans, though less hygienic
and refined, weren't in all likelihood more interesting

and vital than the spinster and her friend. If they were ignorant, it was the ignorance of a primitive folk. These people who held Genesis to be a scientific document and whined over the damnation of the heathen were ignorant by temperament, profession and pigheadedness. I couldn't tear myself away until the party broke up at sunset, because the girls uttered their inanities with such sweet lips and such pallid teeth. But I went home alone through the lovely dusk of Queenshaven and my mind recorded one of the earliest judgments that marked the passing of the boy into the man.

But my growing isolation was more than compensated for by a new joy in thought—its purity and hardihood and strength. My father, wearying of my dogmatic assents, insisted on my reading Fiske's Cosmic Philosophy. I have not seen the book in years. I do not know what I would think of it now. But it was an admirable choice for an awakening intellect. I read it with an icy fervor. A cool, strong light seemed to irradiate my mind. This picture of the universe was so overwhelmingly and evidently nearer the truth than that represented by Christian doctrine that all my emotional forts collapsed at once. I proceeded to read Huxley and Darwin, Draper and Lecky. Yet I held very fast to my faith in God and immortality and I still prayed in the silences of my mind, though I could not have justified the habit on any intellectual basis. Nor did I doubt the correctness and elevation of that system of Christian morals under which we live. In a word, my attitude was that of so many thousands of semi-educated Americans: I was rather proud of my breadth of view on matters of theology and failed quite

to suspect my refusal to think on other matters of far
more pressing practical import. I would have felt
quite at home in that half way house of the mind—
Unitarianism. And indeed, some years later, I did
sustain a brief and tentative connection with that respectable form of faith.

IV

During the last two years of my college course my
plans for the future became more definite. I "majored" in English and having taken all the courses
the college offered, my friend Ferris gave several
courses, both philological and literary, for me alone
and thus enabled me to do a year's graduate work
while I was still an undergraduate. I must emphasize
the fact that both he and several other professors (who
were my thorough friends) aided and encouraged me
in every way and clearly took it for granted that I
would encounter no hardship in entering the academic profession as a teacher of the English language
and literature. My father and mother were also well
content with my plan; their German respect for the
dignity and authority of the academic life increased
their satisfaction.

I can say frankly—since my present self is so far
removed from that old, boyish self in Queenshaven
with its deep faith and ardor—that I prepared myself
for my chosen calling in no common way. I read English literature with a white heat of passion; the lamp
in my bed-room burned dry night after night. By
the time I was nineteen I had read and re-read and
pondered all the great things in English literature

from Chaucer to Kipling, and I had read many authors
of the second and third rank—Jonson and Donne, Mar-
vell and Crashaw, Herrick and Vaughan, Prior and
Gay and Tickell, Collins and Smart, Crabbe and Cow-
per and Hogg, even Bowles and Lloyd, Patmore and
Frederick Tennyson, Clough and Beddoes and Locker-
Lampson down to Lang and Austin Dobson and, of
course, the immediate contemporaries. Yet these
names are but a few and written down at random. The
works of the great poets, even of those who like Lan-
dor are aside from the beaten road, had entered into
my very being. . . . I have had little time to read
English poetry of late years. I do not need to. I
dip into my memory and those immortal numbers
sound upon my inner ear! The early books and the
seventh of Paradise Lost, the Epistle to Augustus,
Adonais and the Nightingale Ode, Kubla Khan and
Work Without Hope, Tintern Abbey and the Ode and
the Sonnets, The Lotos-Eaters and Ulysses, The Last
Ride Together and A Grammarian's Funeral, Thyrsis
and The Scholar Gypsy, The Blessed Damozel and
Jenny, A Forsaken Garden and the elegy on Baude-
laire and the long, dreamy, murmuring melodies—like
the wash of a summer sea—of The Earthly Paradise.
. . . In prose I was not so well grounded. But I knew
the greater prosemen of the eighteenth and nineteenth
centuries, especially my old favorites Swift and Johnson, and the object of my latest and deepest enthusiasm
in college, Matthew Arnold, reasonably well and the
novelists from Fielding to George Eliot intimately.
And I had read all the histories of English literature
available and dozens of volumes of critical essays and
most of the chief biographies from Boswell to Lord

Tennyson's life of his father. Once, when my eyes were being treated, my mother read to me the whole of Dowden's Shelley and of Trevelyan's Macaulay. . . .

I have mentioned Matthew Arnold. My father discovered the volume containing Culture and Anarchy and Friendship's Garland and urged me to read it. I felt the impact of a kindred mind and the book became one of my deepest experiences, although its full import was revealed to me only years later. I read all of Arnold over and over again and I still think him the clearest-souled Englishman of his century. And finally there came—as was inevitable—Pater and Stevenson as the last word in that other great art of prose which I now took almost as seriously as the greater art of verse. I took delight in the tales of Stevenson. But it was characteristic of my youth and its environment that his essays seemed to me not only charmingly written—(they are, though with too obvious a display of dexterity)—but wonderfully rich in wisdom. . . . Recently, at odd moments of leisure, I have been reading Hazlitt again. Almost more than any other English writer he gives, in a voice so little muffled by the grave as almost to ring in one's ears, the deep sense of the texture and savor, the stir and pang of life. Regret and longing, the glory and the disillusion—what poet has rendered them with a more piercing note? Withal his voice is always manly, direct, tempered by some tonic quality within. In my college days I preferred Stevenson. I did not see that Stevenson paints life and feeling in but a few colors. These are bright and very engaging and delicately used. But they fill in a pattern quite arbitrary and unreal. The sentiments and ideals correspond to no well-considered vision of the world. They are like the pipings of some splendid bird in a world all dawn—a world that will never know the heat of noon with its ardor of passion and pain or the dark of night with its contemplation and its faltering hope. . . .

Meanwhile I read both verse and prose, not yielding blindly to the easy and abundant inspiration of youth, but curbing that inspiration and guiding it with severe and fastidious care. The uncriticalness of Southern culture confirmed me in demanding the utmost exactions of myself. There was a terrible lot of facile and amorphous talking and writing. An eighteenth-centuryish type of oratory still throve in Queenshaven. Whenever its echo reached me I re-read Gautier's stanzas on art and tightened the girdle about my loins.

I have recently looked at some thousands of manuscript verses of that period. The poems are full of a rhythmic ardor, yet never without restraint. There are good lines and happy turns of expression and there is no lack of imagination. Yet the stuff is quite worthless. For it is merely, as Arthur Symons wrote me years later (not of my own work) "poetizing about the old subjects in as nearly as possible the old way." There is no directness of speech because there was, after all, no directness of vision. It is all remote and unreal. Mere "literature" in the sense of Verlaine. Without the learned renaissance tradition of English poetry from Surrey to Swinburne the verses were unthinkable. With that tradition and its results extant they were superfluous. But they illustrate how I lived and moved and had my being in the cultural tradition of the Anglo-Saxon aristocrat. I was of those who "speak the tongue that Shakespeare spoke, the faith and morals hold that Milton held" . . .

v.

Does all that sound priggish? It was saved from priggishness, I believe, by its passion, by its inevitableness. There was no blemish of worldly ambition in it all. I thirsted to know, I hungered to create. But I had, all during my sophomore and junior years, another preoccupation, a humbler and, perhaps, a more human one. There was a girl . . . I saw her one day at Sunday School. I met her that week at the Epworth League. Straightway something within me began to ache with a very definite, small, sharp, insistent ache. For two years I had to study very hard or write very feverishly to deaden that pain. Reason and self-persuasion were quite powerless against it. Love at first sight: a very powerful instinct of sexual selection. Each phrase expresses half of the intense reality. The girl was short and rather plump, she had a skin of fine texture, small, white, mouse-like teeth, pale, brown hair, good eyes of grey with long lashes, but a small, prim, cool mouth. She wasn't pretty. Heaven knows she wasn't clever. Her mother and her older sister illustrated with deadly precision what she was certain to become. And I saw all this and nursed no illusions and yet a smile from her would ease me for a day and failure to see her would throw me into helpless agony. I was intensely jealous of her, though I knew her to be quite innocent, not even given to flirting, and though she was obviously anxious to give me every encouragement permitted by a very strict maidenly propriety. What was that chilly preference to my fever and my pain? This experience aroused in me, even in the midst of my suffering, my earliest reflections—vague and inconclusive and rendered futile, of course, by my gentlemanly conservatism—on a tremendous problem. If by any queer and unthinkable chance I could have married the girl, I would have done so—young and penniless and helpless as I was. The knowledge that such a step would have ruined me would not have deterred me for a moment. I wanted her so! It was a good thing, then, that society and custom and parental authority made such a step impossible. On the other hand, it seemed a raw cruelty that the passion of love at its freshest and most vigorous should be a festering spear in the flesh of youth. What a problem! What a world! . . . At the end of the second year I succeeded, by the severest self-discipline, in freeing myself measurably from this torment. I deliberately went out a good deal with a vivid little beauty in whom a quiver of passion constantly fought against but never overcame reserve and principle. She was worth a dozen of the other kind. Yet until I left college I had to avoid that fatal girl with the round shoulders and the dreary mouth lest I should feel again the old, miserable, sickening ache. I marvel how with that scourge upon me I could work so very intensely and continuously. But, though I had next to no worldly ambition, I was anxious to get through college.

I had a deep and urgent motive. I began to see how the Queenshaven life was gradually telling on my father and mother. To my love of them was added a compassion that shook me to the roots of my being and a deadly fear that in my race against time and circumstance, my race for their welfare and their future, I might arrive too late. I began to perceive objectively how the meanness and the humiliations of my father's business were beginning to shake his judgment and to exasperate his moods; how solitariness and repression were whitening my mother's hair. Her face retained its girlish bloom and freshness almost to the threshold of old age. She had hardly a wrinkle when she died. But during my years at college her hair turned quite white and my old terror for her became intensified.

But I must not give the impression that our home life was altogether gloomy. After all we had one another and there were many cheerful hours and days. We were poor but never to the point of penury. A fine care and wise frugality, especially characteristic of my mother, made the modest income suffice for all decent necessities and my studies and development were not interrupted by any material cares. I sometimes thought our diet monotonous. I didn't always like my clothes. But essentially my indifference to such things was quite serene. My father and mother, moreover, were full of hope. My progress was obvious; my teachers constantly impressed upon them the belief that I had an enviable future before me. I had, too, an excellent friend on the Queenshaven Courier, a clever man, almost my father's age, who reprinted my verses in the paper, got me to write articles and book-reviews and so, almost insensibly, I became quite a figure in that small, compact community. . . . How little that meant, how in spite of fair seeming and fair

speech all forces were arrayed against me, I did not
know until several years had passed. . . .

I recall a moonlit, starry night in May. My father
had gone to a lodge meeting. My mother and I paced
the piazza together, as was our wont. It was a few
weeks before my graduation. We spoke long and
quietly of the past and of the future—of my hopes
which seemed well-justified, of the important day that
was coming. We both went to rest, I know, with a real
serenity of soul. . . . More than once later she re-
called that evening to me and asked me whether I
remembered it. Remember it! I shall see those stars
and the shadows on the verandah and her eyes in the
dusk until I see nothing more forever. But the last
time she asked me I feigned forgetfulness. I was beyond all speech. For the hopes had gone down in
shame and frustration and on her face was the mark
of death. . . .

VI.

My graduation was made a notable event in our
small circles. All the leading citizens of the town are
alumni of the college and are proud of its work and
its traditions. So they had followed my writings in the
magazine and in the papers, and when I took two degrees and delivered a commencement oration which,
for once, made some concessions in manner to the more
florid type of Southern oratory, they had a moment of
enthusiasm over me. This enthusiasm was shared by
the press of Queenshaven and by my class-mates. I
was a bit more of a hero than the youth who wins a
series of important foot-ball games for his university.
It was a very great day for me and an even greater

day for my parents: the happiest they had known in years, the happiest they were ever to know again. Under the influence of this wave of communal approbation a board of Episcopal clergymen elected me to the chair of English in a local academy. But the aged clergyman to whom the school really belonged arose from a bed of illness and removed the trustees he had himself appointed for electing a person distasteful to him. He used this expression quite openly in a letter to the Courier. The gentlemen on the board, however, wrote me apologetic letters and my friends and parents agreed that it wasn't, after all, my ambition to teach in a denominational school. Besides, I was only just nineteen and the world seemed all before me where to choose. . . . By Ferris' advice I registered in several teachers' agencies and sent my master's thesis to a scholarly journal by which it was duly accepted for publication.

The long summer weeks dragged on and nothing happened. One New England teachers' agency did, indeed, suggest a place or two but nothing came of my applications. Ferris assured me by letter that this lack of success was due to my youth and inexperience. Since he had councilled me from the first to apply for a fellowship or scholarship in one of the large graduate schools of the east, I accepted his explanation for these happenings as well as for other experiences that came when I applied for school positions within the state. His advice was that I should stay at home for a year, pursue my studies and write a few more scholarly papers to submit with my fellowship applications the following spring. My father, ever the soul of unworldliness in money matters, agreed heartily to this plan and my mother was glad that she could have me with her for another year.

That year stands out in my memory as a pleasant one. I saw little of any one except Ferris, but I was quite free to devote myself to the cultivation of my tastes. And I wrote my first extensive piece of work: an essay in biography and criticism about fifty thousands words in length. Ferris pronounced it well-grounded and well-written—a notable piece of work for a mere youth. So when April came I applied for fellowships at Harvard and Columbia and both Ferris and I were hopeful of the results. From both universities, however, I received only pleasant acknowledgements of the work I had sent in support of my applications, an invitation to pursue my graduate studies and regrets that neither a fellowship nor a scholarship were available. This was a hard blow. It was obvious that I could not go on living on my father's kindness. On the contrary, I was passionately anxious to help him and my mother to free themselves from the bonds of their Queenshaven life. I did not speak of this, for I did not want to render their consciousness of it more acute. But it weighed on me heavily. I thought and thought and came to a resolve which many American youths take lightly enough, but which cost me infinite hesitation and pain: I would borrow money. The notion of working my way through the graduate course never occurred to me. For I was not concerned with text-books or, primarily, with degrees, but with a life to be lived, an absorption and dedication to be accomplished. And this never presented itself to my mind as possible upon any terms but those of a complete release from sordid preoccupations.

Unhappily for me the wealthy Jewish physician of my Methodist days had recently died. Had he been alive my way would have been easier. I felt close to him and he was kind and generous. As it was, I had to go to other prominent citizens and alumni of the college. These men had all liked me and made much of me for years; I felt quite at home with them in all essential matters and yet it was a terrible struggle. I put off my errand from day to day; I went to the door of some office and hadn't the courage to enter. A sensation of physical nausea and of burning shame overwhelmed me. . . . I have never been able to feel differently. If I must ask for something, however clear my right to make the demand or the request, the old, sickening misery comes over me and I am helpless, stupid, stammering, absurd. For the sake of others I have had to ask things since then. For myself I would never have the strength to face that sense of spiritual nakedness and abasement. Perhaps it is from this native feeling that there has grown my passion for justice. The more just we are to our fellowmen, the less need we wound and degrade them with our wretched mercy. True justice—I do not mean the tribal terrors or capitalistic voracities of our legal and moral codes—true justice need not be tempered by mercy. It excludes the necessity for mercy. You do not need to be merciful until you have ceased to be just. . .!

The Queenshaven gentlemen, it is but fair to add, made my dreadful task comparatively easy. Several of them met to discuss the matter and made up for me a loan of three hundred and fifty dollars. I had really wanted six hundred to see me through the year at

Columbia, since the tuition alone was a hundred and fifty. But wild horses, in the vivid old phrase, could have dragged no further begging from my lips. I thanked them with what grace I could master and proceeded to get ready for my great adventure.

Let any one who has an unclouded vision of our American life, and not least of the academic part of it, consider my undertaking. How often since have I reflected on it, sometimes in a mood of bitterness, sometimes in one of irony. I had lived utterly for the things of the mind and the emotions. I was twenty years old and knew less of practical matters than many a child of ten. I had no social adroitness but the most quivering sensitiveness and pride. I was passionately Anglo-American in all my sympathies, I wanted above all things to be a poet in the English tongue, and my name and physiognomy were characteristically Jewish. I had ill-cut, provincial clothes and just money enough to get through one semester. Such was my inner and outer equipment for pursuing in a metropolitan graduate school the course which was to lead to a college appointment to teach English. No one warned me, no one discouraged me. It seems incredible that Ferris had no inkling of the quality of my undertaking. But he, too, kept silent. So I faced the future with a steady hopefulness. Only when I sought to grasp what separation from my mother would mean to her and me did my heart sink. We tried to comfort each other, she and I, by dwelling upon the certainty of a successful career for myself. But during the last days we gave up these feeble and hollow efforts and fell quite silent before our unavertible fate.

CHAPTER V.

The American Discovers Exile.

I.

In those days the steamers from the South landed at piers on the North River. I was too deeply preoccupied with that first, tremendous, lonely plunge into the world to watch the harbor or the sky-line of New York. I stood on deck, grasping my valise tightly, holding my hat. The sharp wind was full of scurries of rain. It was almost dark when we passengers trickled across the plank into the appalling mud of the streets. The lower West side is, I still think, the dismallest port of the city. On that day, coming from the bland and familiar South and from a life that touched reality so feebly, it seemed brutal, ferocious, stark. . . . An indifferent acquaintance met me and hustled me to the nearest station of the Ninth Avenue "L." We climbed the iron staircase, scrambled for tickets and were jammed into a car. It was the evening rush hour and we had barely standing room. The train rattled on its way to Harlem. At One Hundred and Sixteenth Street we slid down in the elevator to the street, frantically dodged people and vehicles across Eighth Avenue, turned south and west and stood presently before one of a row of three story houses wedged in between huge, dark buildings. My guide introduced me to the boarding-house keeper, a hard-featured, heavily rouged woman who seemed in pain and in a hurry. They led me to a hall bedroom on the third floor, lit a whirring gas-jet and, in another minute, were gone. I put down my valise and took off my overcoat and stood still, quite still, between the bed and the chiffonier. I could touch one with either hand. I was in New York. I was alone.

At such moments one's intentions to conquer the world avail little. Especially if one is twenty. I heard the far away roar of New York like the roar of a sinister and soulless machine that drags men in and crunches them between its implacable wheels. It seemed to me that I would never be able to face it. I huddled in that small, cold room in an old traveling robe of my father's and bit my lips. But I had the manhood not to write home in that mood. Indeed my old stoicism had not deserted me and my parents never learned of the grinding misery of my first weeks in New York.

In the morning the October sun shone. At breakfast the landlady seemed not nearly so menacing. I may add at once that she was an intelligent and courageous woman who had suffered much and undeservedly and that we became great friends. She gave me on that first day what simple directions I needed. I left the house, walked to the corner and turned my face toward the west. Morningside Heights with its many poplars rose sheer against a sparkling autumn sky. The beauty of it seemed much colder to me that day than it does now. But it was beauty—something to dwell with, to calm and to console the mind. I took heart at once and climbed the heights and presently came upon the approach to the University library. The river shone still farther to the west, with the russet palisades beyond. But I hastened across the quadrangle, eager for some human contact in this new world full of cold power and forbidding brilliance.

Professor Brent of the department of English, with whom I had had some correspondence, received me with a winning kindliness. We had a talk the other day and I observed him and remembered the old days. He has grown grayer. Otherwise he is the same—the lank, unathletic but not graceless form, the oblong head lengthened by a pointed beard, the pleasant, humorous but powerful glance, the easy pose, tilted back in his chair, the eternal cigarette between his long, bony, sensitive fingers. A scholarly and poetic figure, languid enough, but capable of a steady tenacity at the urge of some noble passion of the mind. That he was a trenchant and intrepid thinker I always knew. How magnificently he would stand the ultimate intellectual test of this, or perhaps, any age, I was to learn much later. . . . He introduced me to Brewer, secretary of the department, a pale, hesitant, chill-eyed New Englander with a thin strain of rhetorical skill and literary taste.

German was to be my second "minor", largely because it would be easy and would give me more time for my English studies. And so I went to present myself to Professor Richard who had also written me a pleasant letter. I found him tall, erect, frugal and incisive of speech, a spirit of great rectitude, of a purity almost too intense to grasp the concrete forces and passions of the fevered world; clear, high-souled, a little passionless, but all that without effort or prigishness. His intellectual and artistic sympathies were, of course, limited. But within its limits his was an admirable and a manly mind.

The qualities of Brent and Richard did not, of course, reveal themselves to me at once. Nor, indeed, for long thereafter and then in private interviews and at club-meetings. The lectures of these excellent professors were dull and dispiriting to me. I found in them no living sustenance of any sort. For years I sought to grasp the reasons for this fact. I do not think I grasped them wholly until I myself began to lecture to graduate students and to have such students in my own seminar. I came to the university with the reading I have described. I knew all the books that one was required to know in the various lecture courses. What I wanted was ideas, interpretative, critical, aesthetic, philosophical, with which to vivify, to organize, to deepen my knowledge, on which to nourish and develop my intellectual self. And my friends, the professors, ladled out information. Poor men, how could they help it? I thought in those days that all graduate students knew what I and a small group of my friends knew. I am aware now of the literally incredible ignorance of the average bachelors of our colleges. . . . I cannot, of course, absolve the professors entirely, though only the rigorous veracity that gives its meaning to this narrative can force me to admit even so much of friends who have stood by me so long and so wholeheartedly as Brent and Richard. They did not give themselves enough, nor freely enough. They did not realize that, the elementary tools of knowledge once gained, there is but one thing that can teach men and that is the play of a large and an incisive personality. In a word, I was an ardent disciple and I found no master. So I drifted and occasionally "cut" lectures and wrote my reports and passed creditable examinations without doing a page of the required reading. I had done it all! I read for myself in entirely new directions—books that changed the whole tenor of my inner life—and struggled to make a living and wrote verses and walked and talked and sat in bar-rooms and cheap eating-houses with my friend Ellard—my friend of friends, whom I found at this time and who is still *animae dimidium meae.*

II.

It was a grey, windy November forenoon that we first talked on the steps of Fayerwether Hall. He was tall and lank and thin to emaciation. An almost ragged overcoat fluttered behind him, a shapeless, discolored hat tilted a little on his head. His delicate nostrils seemed always about to quiver, his lips to be set in a half-petulant, half-scornful determination. From under the hat shone two of the most eloquent eyes—fiery and penetrating, gloomy and full of laughter in turn—that were ever set in a human head. He spoke with large, loose, expressive gestures and with a strange, abrupt way of ending his sentences. I felt drawn to him at once. Freedom and nobility seemed to clothe him and a stoic wildness. A young eagle with plumage ruffled by the storm. . . . ! I asked him, I don't know why, whether he wrote verse. And when he said that he did I knew instinctively that his verses were better than mine, far better, and curiously enough I was not sorry but glad and, in a way, elated. I cannot tell at this distance of time how rapidly our friendship ripened, but I know that we soon saw a great deal of each other.

He lived in a small, crowded room up four flights of stairs. A large kerosene lamp stood on his study table. A sharp, triangular shadow lay steadily across bed and wall. He was tormented by poverty and love and by the intellectual bleakness that was all about us. For two years he had been at Bonn and though by blood a New England Brahmin of the purest strain, the sunny comradeship and spiritual freedom of the Rhineland city had entered into his very being. I see him standing there in the blue cloud of our cigarette-smoke chanting me his verses. I had never met a poet before and poetry meant everything to me in those days. A lovely or a noble line, a sonorous or a troubling turn of rhythm could enchant me for days. So that I was wholly carried away by my friend and his poems. And we both felt ourselves to be in some sort exiles and wandered the streets as the fall deepened into winter, engaged in infinite talk. We watched as evening came the bursting of the fiery blooms of light over the city and again, late at night, met in some eating house or bar-room on Amsterdam Avenue where the belated, frozen car men watched us with heavy curiosity. We found ourselves then, as we have found ourselves ever since, in complete harmony as to the deeper things in life. That that harmony has become, if anything, more entire during the past seven crucial years of the world's history, I account as one of the few sustaining factors in my life and to it I attach, not foolishly I think, an almost mystical significance. . . .

I have been re-reading his poetry. I can detach it quite coldly now from the romance of our early commadeship, from the comforts of our maturer friendship. Nor am I as easily stirred as I was once. It is inferior to no poetry that has been written on this continent. At its best it is at least equal to the noblest passages of Emerson and it is far less fragmentary, far more sustained upon an extraordinary level of intellectual incisiveness, moral freedom and untraditional beauty. And there are many lines and passages that in their imagination and passion and wisdom cleave so deeply to the tragic core of life that they might bring tears to the eyes of grave and disillusioned men. . . . What has it availed him? His volumes scarcely sell; the manuscript of his third one is being hawked about from publisher to publisher. His verse is handicapped by its intellectual severity and its disdain of fashion—the poetic fashion of either yesterday or to-day. But it has the accent of greatness and that is bound to tell in the long run.

Other friendships there were for me at the university, pleasant enough at that time, but all impermanent save one more. I still count George Fredericks, sober-minded, virile, generous, among my chosen comrades. And I still think, with much kindness, of G. now a college professor in the East, a fine, pure spirit, a New Englander like Ellard, but unlike him striving quite in vain to transcend the moral and intellectual parochialism of his section and his blood. But, indeed, I sought no companionship, taking only such as came my way. For mean anxieties soon beset me as my slender borrowings came to an end and I tramped the streets in search of tutoring. A crowd of queer and colorful and

comic scenes—sorrowful and humiliating enough at
that time—floats into my mind. In a gorgeous palace
near Central Park the footman eyed me contemptu-
ously and an elderly woman tried to hire me to conduct her evidently rowdy boys to and from school. I
refused curtly to do a nurse-maid's work. But walking
across the rich carpet to the door I heard my torn
shoes make a squdgy sound and almost repented. In
another elaborate establishment I gave, in a very
ready-made Louis XV room a single lesson to the
young daughter of the house. Next day a note came
dispensing with my services. I wasn't surprised. The
girl was pretty and I was hungry for charm and love
and she had evidently not disliked me. . . . At last I
got a couple of boys to tutor (one a deaf-mute) and
lessons in scientific German to give to the staff of one
of the city institutions. Two evenings a week I was
ferried across Hellgate in the icy wind to give this
instruction. It was a bleak and tiresome business, but
it paid room and board and tobacco and an occasional
glass of beer.

III

Meanwhile I read the nights away. Fascinating
hints had come to me in Queenshaven, despite my
whole-souled absorption in English literature, of certain modern German plays and poems and novels
which seemed, by all reports, to differ wonderfully
from both Schiller and Heine, the two German poets
whom I knew best, and also from such popular mid-
century writers as Scheffel and Heyse. But very few
German books ever made their way to Queenshaven.

Here, in the University library, I found them all and I read them all.

I read them with joy, with a sense of liberation, with a feeling that no other books in the world had ever given me. I struggled against that feeling; I seemed to myself almost disloyal to the modern English masters, to the very speech that I loved and which I hoped to write notably some day. But a conviction came upon me after some months with irresistible force. All or nearly all English books since Fielding were literature. This was life. All or nearly all the English literature by which our generation lives is, in substance, rigidly bounded within certain intellectual and ethical categories. This was freedom. I now understood my old, instinctive love for the prosemen of the eighteenth century. They had the sense for life —a life remote from ours, to be sure—but their sense of it was manly and incorruptible. In Wordsworth and in Tennyson I found substantially the same elevated sentiments. Except in the narrow field of the religious emotions, they and their contemporaries had no sense for reality at all, only for pseudo-nobility. And in English fiction, in 1904, all the people really held the same elevated sentiments, sentiments which were mostly false and unnecessary, and of course couldn't and didn't live up to them. They were all like poor Byron who half believed that one ought to be a Christian and a church-going householder and who was romantically desperate over his own wicked nature. Or they were like the slim, pale-eyed son of my old Sunday school superintendent. The lad had an excellent tenor voice and joined a small opera company. On one of his visits home he said to me with a troubled look in his eyes: "I don't see why I should be this way. My father's such a good man." . . . Of course I'm stating the case crassly and unjustly as one always does and must for the sake of emphasis. And, of course, I shall be held, whatever I say, to be approving a drifting with the passions of human life—like that of Burns—instead of an understanding and use and mastery of them. But it will not be denied by any really honest and penetrating thinker that English literature from Fielding until quite recently was curiously remote from life, curiously helpless and unhelpful and yet arrogant in the face of it. Such books as Moore's Esther Waters, which I hadn't read, and Wells' The Passionate Friends, which hadn't yet been written, have introduced into English letters an entirely new element of spiritual veracity and moral freedom. And these were the qualities which I found so pervasively and overwhelmingly present (yet with no lack of beauty and music in structure and style) in modern German literature. If in these books there was a noble sentiment it was there because it had grown inevitably from the sweat and tears, the yearning and the aspiration of our mortal fate—it was never set down because it was a correct sentiment to which human nature must be made to conform. I understood very fully now the saying of that character in one of Henry James' stories: "When I read a novel, it's usually a French one. You get so much more life for your money." I read French books, too. But compared to the German ones they seemed, as they are, rather hard and monotonous and lacking in spiritual delicacy. . . . Someone gave me a copy of Hans Benzmann's anthology of the modern German lyric. I found there an immediate rendering of life into art, not mere isolated elements of it selected according to a tradition of pseudo-nobility and then fixed in the forms of post-Renaissance culture. The pangs and aspirations of my own heart—and of all hearts, if men would but be honest among us—were here, the haunting echoes of my inner life, the deep things, the true things of which I had been ashamed and which I had tried to transmute into the correct sentiments of my Anglo-American environment—I found them all in the lyrical charm of these poets, in their music, which is the very music of the mind, in their words, which are the very words of life. They spoke my thoughts, they felt my conflicts; they dared to be themselves—these modern men and women who were impassioned and troubled like myself, who had not snared the universe in barren formulae, but who were seekers and strivers! They didn't know the whole duty of man; they didn't try to huddle out of sight the eternal things that make us what we are; they hadn't reduced the moral and spiritual life of the race to a series of gestures of more than Egyptian rigidity. They made me free; they set me on the road of trying to be not what was thought correct without reference to reality, but what I was naturally meant to be. They taught me, not directly, but by the luminous implications of their works, the complete spiritual unveracity in which I had been living and in which most of my Anglo-American friends seemed to be living. . . . This whole process was, of course, very gradual on its practical or outer side. Within me, too, the old ready-made formulae would often arise to inhibit or torment me. And from this conflict and turbidness of feeling and vision there sprang some grave errors of action.

But that was because my freedom was not yet a rational freedom, nor one corrected by a power of rational experience. My youth had been passed amid so much falseness that my mastery of fact was quite inadequate for the practice of a real moral freedom. I had no way at all of seeing things as they really are, no power of measuring the origin and direction of the forces that rule men and the world. I was like someone to whom is offered the freedom of a great library, but who had been deliberately mistaught the meaning of the symbols in which the books are written. I knew that it was my duty now to read for myself. I didn't know how to read. I am struggling to express a difficult and momentous truth: The young creators of new values come to grief so often not because their values are wrong, nor because their rebellion is not of the very breath of the world's better life. They come to grief because they have no mastery of fact, because they carry with them the false old interpretations and conventional idealizations of man, and nature, and human life. . . . Nevertheless the world now opened itself to me in a new guise. I had been accustomed, as I had been taught, to approve and to disapprove. Now for the first time I watched life honestly and lost myself in it and became part of it with my soul and my sympathies, detached only in the citadel of the analytic and recording, never more of the judging mind. I became aware of faces—the faces of people on the streets, in the cars, in the subway. And I no longer thought of people as good and bad or desirable or undesirable, but I saw in all faces the struggle and the passion and the sorrow, sometimes ugly, unheroic enough always by the old, foolish tests, but full of endless fascination. . . .

To a modern Continental, French or German or Italian, this whole matter will seem primitive and absurd. He may be sure that I am touching on the central weakness of the Anglo-American mind—its moral illusionism. That mind is generally quite sincere. It really arranges its own impulses and the impulses of other men in a rigid hierarchy of fixed norms. It has surrendered the right and the power of examining the contents of such concepts as "right," "wrong," "pure," "democracy," "liberty," "progress," or of bringing these conventionalized gestures of the mind to the test of experience. It has not, indeed, ever naively experienced anything. For it holds the examination of an experience in itself, and without reference to an anterior and quite rigid norm to be a "sin." It hides the edges of the sea of life with a board-walk of ethical concepts and sits there, hoping that no one will hear the thunder of the surf of human passions on the rocks below. . . .

IV

A face, a voice, a gesture that seemed strange and unheard of arose before me and I was stricken by a blind and morbid passion. All the repressions of my tormented adolescence, all the false inhibitions in thought and deed now went toward the nourishing of this hectic bloom. It was winter. A white and silent winter. Playing with curious fancies we called our passion roses in the snow. I committed every extravagance and every folly. I knew nothing of life, nothing of human nature. I knew ethical formulae which, obviously, didn't apply—that were, at best, vicious half-truths. Thus all the defences of my soul broke down. I had never been taught a sane self-direction. The repetition of tribal charms which were quite external had been deemed a sufficient safeguard. Happily, though my passion was morbid enough and caused me untold suffering, it was blended with the love of letters and with a keen though unwholesome romance. There was nothing in it of baseness, nothing of degradation. I am not proud of it but I am not ashamed of it. I look back upon it and it blends, in strange tones, into the inevitable music of life—neither good nor evil, neither right nor wrong. We are both married now and meet in pleasant friendship and remember half-humorously that long ago—so long ago, it seems a fairy-tale—we caused each other delights and pangs and tears. . . .

But if I had a son I should say to him: "Dismiss from your mind all the cant you hear on the subject of sex. The passion of love is the central passion of human life. It should be humanized; it should be made beautiful. It should never be debased by a sense that it is in itself sinful, for that is to make the whole of life sinful and to corrupt our human experience at its very source. Love is not to be condemned and so degraded, but to be exercised and mastered. If you are of a cool temper and continence leaves your mind serene and your imagination unbesmirched, very well. But let not your soul, if it is ardent, become contaminated and disordered by false shames and a false sense of sin. Love in itself is the source of loveliness and wisdom if it is gratified without falsehood and without abandoning the sterner elements of life. Natural things are made sinful only by a mistaken notion that they are so. Account love, then, as inevitable and lovely, but remain master of your soul and of yourself and of the larger purposes which you were born to fulfill.''

To me, as to every American youth, it had been said: ''Passion, except within marriage, is the most degrading of sins. Within marriage it is forgiven but never mentioned as being, even there, unmentionable. This is the law.'' Meantime all the men and youths I knew slunk into the dark alleys of Queenshaven whither I did not follow them. And curiously, in that very act, they still believed the follies they proclaimed. They were simply moral men sinning against their own convictions. That astonishing ethical dualism of the English mind—(so truly and so moderately set forth by George Gissing in the memorable twentieth chapter of the third book of The Private Papers of Henry Ryecroft)—that ethical duality of conscience I hold the chief and most corrupting danger of our life as a people. It must be fought without ceasing and without mercy. . . .

Of that duality there was nothing in my being. I was bound or I was free. But having been a slave so long I ran amuck in my freedom and in the recoil came almost to utter grief. I was saved and made steadfast only by the thought of those two watchers in the distant South. However absorbed in that most passionate adventure, I never missed an opportunity of going home at Christmas or even at Easter—planned for it, saved for it, and always my mother's hand in mine and her eyes upon me made me well again.

Also I could now conquer many moods and free myself from them by fixing them in art. My verse was no longer the echo of a sonorous tradition. It grew no longer out of the love of poetry but out of the pain of life. And from my modern Germans as well as from a new and powerful movement in our English verse I learned to write directly and truly. Somehow, in Queenshaven, I had missed a poem which is not, of course, the greatest, but assuredly the most important English poem of the third quarter of the nineteenth century: Meredith's Modern Love. The application of English poetic art to the actual, the contemporary and the real had there been inaugurated. In addition I now read Henley and Housman's A Shropshire Lad and The Love Sonnets of Proteus and, above all, I found the two-volume edition of the poems of Arthur Symons. Granting the hostile critic his monotony of mood (but is not Shelley's mood quite as monotonous in a different spiritual key?), and his morbidness (though what *is* morbidness, after all?) and there remains in his work the creation of a new style, a new method, a new power. The conventional taste of his generation still lags behind his method, but in it is one of the essential forces of the future of English poetry.

V

The various experiences which I have set down so briefly extended over two years. At the end of the first year I duly took my master's degree and applied for a fellowship. Among the group of students to which I belonged it was taken for granted that, since Ellard had completed his studies for the doctorate, I would undoubtedly be chosen. I record this, heaven knows, not from motives of vanity but as part of the subtler purpose of this story. The faculty elected my friend G. I went, with a heavy heart, to interview Professor Brewer, not to push my claims to anything, but because I was at my wits' end. I dreaded another year of tutoring and of living wretchedly from hand to mouth, without proper clothes, without books. Brewer leaned back in his chair, pipe in hand, with a cool and kindly smile. "It seemed to us," he stuttered, "that the university hadn't had its full influence on you." He suggested their disappointment in me and, by the subtlest of stresses, their sorrow over this disappointment. I said that I had been struggling for a livelihood and that, nevertheless, my examinations had uniformly received high grades and my papers, quite as uniformly, the public approval of Brent and himself. He avoided a direct answer by explaining that the department had recommended me for a scholarship for the following year. The truth is, I think, that Brewer, excessively mediocre as he was, had a very keen tribal instinct of the self-protective sort and felt in me—what I was hardly yet consciously—the implacable foe of the New England dominance over our national life. I wasn't unaware of his hostility, but I had no way of provoking a franker explanation.

I forgot my troubles in three beautiful months at home—three months seemed so long then—or, rather, I crowded these troubles from my field of consciousness. I wouldn't even permit the fact that I wasn't elected to a scholarship to depress me. Brewer wrote a letter of regret and encouragement that was very kindly in tone. The pleasant implication of that letter was, of course, a spiritual falsehood of the crassest. He knew then precisely what he knew and finally told me ten months later. But his kind has a dread of the bleak weather of the world of truth, and approaches it gingerly, gradually, with a mincing gait. He, poor man, was probably unconscious of all that. In him, as in all like him, the corruption of the mental life is such that the boundaries between the true and the false are wholly obliterated.

In the passionate crises of the second year I often walked as in a dream. And I was encouraged by the fact that the department arranged a loan for my tuition. In truth, I was deeply touched by so unusual a kindness and I feel sure that the suggestion came from Brent. If so, Brewer again did me a fatal injury by not preventing that kindness. For he had then, I must emphasize, the knowledge he communicated to me later—the knowledge that held the grim upshot of my university career.

Spring came and with it the scramble for jobs among the second year men. My friends were called in to conferences with Brewer; I was not. They discussed vacancies, chances here and there. It wasn't the chagrin that hurt so; it wasn't any fear for myself. After all I was only twenty-two and I was careless of material things. I thought of my father and my mother in the cruel sunshine of Queenshaven. Their hope and dream and consolation were at stake. I could see them, not only by day, but in the evening, beside their solitary lamps, looking up from their quiet books, thinking of me and of the future. . . . I remembered how my father had believed in certain implications of American democracy. I remembered

. . . I was but a lad, after all. I couldn't face Brewer's cool and careless smile. I wrote him a letter—a letter which, in its very earnestness and passionate veracity must have struck like a discord upon the careful arrangements of his safe and proper nature. For in it I spoke of grave things gravely, not jestingly, as one should to be a New England gentleman: I spoke of need and aspiration and justice. His answer lies before me now and I copy that astonishingly smooth and chilly document verbatim: "It is very sensible of you to look so carefully into your plans at this juncture, because I do not at all believe in the wisdom of your scheme. A recent experience has shown me how terribly hard it is for a man of Jewish birth to get a good position. I had always suspected that it was a matter worth considering, but I had not known how wide-spread and strong it was. While we shall be glad to do anything we can for you, therefore, I cannot help feeling that the chances are going to be greatly against you."

I sat in my boarding-house room playing with this letter. I seemed to have no feeling at all for the moment. By the light of a sunbeam that fell in I saw that the picture of my parents on the mantelpiece was very dusty. I got up and wiped the dust off carefully. Gradually an eerie, lost feeling came over me. I took my hat and walked out and up Amsterdam Avenue, farther and farther to High Bridge and stood on the bridge and watched the swift, tiny tandems on the Speedway below and the skiffs gliding up and down the Harlem River. A numbness held my soul and mutely I watched life, like a dream pageant, float by me. . . . I ate nothing till evening when I went into a bakery and, catching sight of myself in a mirror, noted with dull objectivity my dark hair, my melancholy eyes, my unmistakably Semitic nose. . . . An outcast. . . . A sentence arose in my mind which I have remembered and used ever since. So long as there is discrimination, there is exile. And for the first time in my life my heart turned with grief and remorse to the thought of my brethren in exile all over the world. . . .

VI

The subconscious self has a tough instinct of self-preservation. It thrusts from the field of vision, as Freud has shown, the painful and the hostile things of life. Thus I had forgotten, except at moments of searching reflection, the social fate of my father and mother, my failure to be elected to the fraternity at college, and other subtler hints and warnings. I had believed the assertion and made it myself that equality of opportunity was implicit in the very spiritual foundations of the Republic. This is what I wanted to believe, what I needed to believe in order to go about the business of my life at all. I had listened with a correct American scorn to stories of how some distant kinsman in Germany, many years ago, had had to receive Christian baptism in order to enter the consular service of his country. At one blow now all these delusions were swept away and the facts stood out in the sharp light of my dismay. Discrimination there was everywhere. But a definite and public discrimination is, at least, an enemy in the open. In pre-war Germany, for instance, no Jew could be prevented from entering the academic profession. Unless he was very brilliant and productive his promotion was less rapid than that of his Gentile colleagues. He knew that and reckoned with it. He knew, too, for instance, that he could not become senior professor of German at Berlin (only associate professor like the late R. M. Meyer), nor Kultusminister, but he could become a full professor of Latin or philosophy, and, of course, of all the sciences. I am not defending these restrictions and I think the argument for them—that the German state was based upon an ethnic homogeneity which corresponds to a spiritual oneness—quite specious. I am contrasting these conditions with our own. We boast our equality and freedom and call it Americanism and speak of other countries with disdain. And so one is unwarned, encouraged and flung into the street. With exquisite courtesy, I admit. And the consciousness of that personal courtesy soothes the minds of our Gentile friends. . . . It will be replied that there are a number of Jewish scholars in American colleges and universities. There are. The older men got in because nativistic anti-Semitism was not nearly as strong twenty-five years ago as it is to-day. Faint remnants of the ideals of the early Republic still lingered in American life. But in regard to the younger men I dare to assert that in each case they were appointed through personal friendship, family or financial prestige or some other abnormal relenting of the iron prejudice which is the rule. But that prejudice has not, to my knowledge, relented in a single instance in regard to the teaching of English. So that our guardianship of the native tongue is far fiercer than it is in an, after all, racially homogeneous state like Germany. Presidents, deans and departmental heads deny this

fact or gloss it over in public. Among themselves it
is admitted as a matter of course.

I have not touched the deeper and finer issues,
though I have written in vain if they are not clear.
My purest energy and passion, my best human aspirations had been dedicated from my earliest years to a
given end. It was far more than a question of bread
and butter, though it was that too. I didn't know how
to go on living a reasonable and reasonably harmon-
ious inner life. I could take no refuge in the spirit and
traditions of my own people. I knew little of them.
My psychical life was Aryan through and through.
Slowly, in the course of the years, I have discovered
traits in me which I sometimes call Jewish. But that
interpretation is open to grave doubt. I can, in reality,
find no difference between my own inner life of
thought and impulse and that of my very close friends
whether American or German. So that the picture of
a young man disappointed because he can't get the
kind of a job he wants, doesn't exhaust, barely indeed
touches the dilemma. I didn't know what to do with
my life or with myself.

In this matter of freedom and equality and democratic justice, then, I found in my Anglo-American
world precisely that same strange dualism of conscience which I had discovered there in the life of sex.
The Brewers in the academic world do truly believe
that our society is free and democratic. When they
proclaim that belief at public banquets a genuine emotion fills their hearts. Just as a genuine emotion filled
the hearts of my Southern friends (who used Mulatto
harlots) when in the interest of purity and the home

they refused to sanction the enactment of any divorce law in their native state.

I do not wish to speak bitterly or flippantly. I am approaching the analysis of thoughts and events beside which my personal fate is less than nothing. And I need but think of my Queenshaven youth or of some passage of Milton or Arnold, or of those tried friendships that are so large a part of the unalterable good of life, or of the bright hair and gray English eyes of my own wife to know that I can never speak as an enemy of the Anglo-Saxon race. But unless that race abandons its duality of conscience, unless it learns to honor and practice a stricter spiritual veracity, it will either destroy civilization through disasters yet unheard of or sink into a memory and into the shadow of a name.

CHAPTER VI

The American Finds Refuge

I

In my confusion of mind I didn't revise my dissertation and left the university without my doctor's degree. Brent was angry at this and I remember a scene in his study. He strode up and down and rebuked me with a sternness that showed his friendship toward me. I sat huddled in a chair. I couldn't bear to tell him what was going on within me. Whether he guessed it or not, he made every effort to find me some suitable employment. I suspect that he actually walked the glaring streets that early summer from office to office. He got me a sub-editorship on one of those huge compilation sets which people seem to buy—queer kinds of people that one never meets—and, one hopes, read with profit. And this employment led, in the course of a few months, to a position on the editorial staff of Singleton, Leaf and Company.

In the meantime I went home, joylessly for the first time. The glaring fact couldn't be hidden. I had no academic position, however humble. Here, too, the evil unveracity of early influences crippled my soul. It was generally agreed that there *was* no Anti-Semitism in America. It had been held un-American to assert that there was. . . . So I even permitted my father to suspect that I had, perhaps, neglected my studies. I said that I preferred the career of letters. "But this is hack-work," he retorted. "It's a beginning," I declared lamely, "I'm only twenty-two." My mother felt that a shadow lay subtly between us. It seemed to me—foolishly, I know now—that I could not offer her the affront of saying that I was doomed to this failure because I was her child. . . . A special delivery letter came recalling me to New York. I didn't want to go, I wanted to beg my father to let me stay and think and plan some other future. But I had grown up among a dumb folk who hold it ill-bred to have a troubled heart; I had tried so hard to be like them, for the love of their art, that I had gained no power over life or speech. . . .

Often and often, in subsequent years, when I was irked by the unresponsiveness of students or tired of lecturing, the thought flashed through my mind: For all that, thank Heaven, it's not Singleton, Leaf and Company. I can, at least, see the sun and think my own thoughts. And there arises in me the memory of that large, scientifically clean building filled with the hum of the engine that drove the monotype machine and with the acrid odor of fresh print. A sharp electric light burned over my desk from eight-thirty to twelve-thirty and from one-thirty to five-thirty, and next to me stood all day a long, loose fellow whose small, pointed head seemed fairly to dangle and tremble, like an ugly and noxious flower, at the end of his scrawny neck. He was constantly in a Uriah Heepish ecstasy of contortion over the greatness of the firm we served and the huge increases in advertising matter to be "made up" for its magazines month by month. This man and his green-eyed leer—there was something coldly lecherous in it—became to me a symbol of my degradation. For it was degradation. Singleton, Leaf and Company did not consciously or purposefully publish a line for its literary or scientific value. The stuff was accepted or, more often, arranged for merely that it might sell. It did. But the business had no more to do with literature or science (except by accident: occasionally good work will sell), than a breakfast food factory. The firm had its own special ideals, to be sure. It accepted and then refused to publish Dreiser's first great book. But except for this gentlemanly avoidance of sex in literature, it had no prejudices. It published, in my time, a most slanderous and ignorant piece of Anti-Semitic propaganda. Nor was any book or article too shoddy, too ill-written, too superficial to put more money into the purses of Singleton and Leaf. So far, so good. In our predatory economic system such was the clear right of these gentlemen. But why the odious corruption of which my pitiful and shabby neighbor was the sign and symbol? Why "get together luncheons" for the firm's employees with speeches and base rhetoric and brazen enthusiasm? Enthusiasm for the ill-gotten gains of Singleton and Leaf! They were the masters and we were the men. Very well. Why this unctuous lying, this degrading of the souls of the wage-slave? The proletarian printers were far more self-respecting in this matter than the business and editorial employees who fawned and "enthused" (vile word for a vile thing) over the growth of the business. . . . Later I often gave the best that was in me and often the last ounce of my strength for a wretched wage. But I served the spiritual common-weal in no ignoble way. And I could have served that common-weal in a far humbler office with my human dignity unimpaired. The meanest door-keeper in the house of the Republic still serves—the Republic. There should not be money enough in the world to hire any self-sustaining man to minister to the voracities of those whose aims are alien from his own and commonly demonstrably sinister. When former students of mine tell me that they are "making good" with this corporation or that and boast of the power and wealth of those corporations, a sense of bleakness fills me. The humble digger of the earth may be a slave in body; the young business man or engineer who furthers the interests of his master is a slave in soul.

All summer, a great and flaring summer, I watched the tramps and "pan-handlers" on Union Square during my luncheon hour. They dozed over stray newspapers and smoked remnants of tobacco in disreputable pipes. They fascinated me—their white, unshaven faces, reddish eyes, frayed coats, ripped boots. They stared at me—careless, unashamed, imperturbable . . . free, in that they had cast off responsibility and subservience. Types of the eternal beggar, the outcast, the rebel, the unquiet one. He was beside the gates of Niniveh—as in Union Square. But most of us have an undying house-dweller and even householder within us. We need warmth and security and respect. Especially when we are young. Yet I understood the temptation of stepping out of the ranks and drifting off into the land of unconsidered men. . . . I understood it so well that I openly and frankly, at

Singleton, Leaf and Company's, showed my sense of the absurdity and vulgarity of the whole business. So the firm set me down as an able but queer and un-ambitious person—one that sensible people could make nothing of—and we parted on friendly enough terms. I still have a letter of recommendation that Leaf gave me. It seems queer and remote and unreal. It did me little good.

But I met Mary that year. . . . Bread came some-how. I wrote stuff for the Review of Reviews and articles for the Times and she wrote verses for it. I sold some poems to Collier's. We had each other. . . . I recall September days full of a soft, grey drizzle. The lights of the street-lamps trembled in a thousand rays through the wet air. But we, under one umbrella, recked little of the world. The weather cleared and brightened as October came. We lingered on River-side Drive and heard the rustle of the leaves under our feet and waited until the sun set in a bronze haze over the palisades. We sat on a bench under the bare pop-lars with all the stars of heaven for our own. We were, of course, aware of the necessary briefness of this period, but we dwelt with all our might in the days and hours—numbered days and hours—that were given us. The windfalls grew fewer and fewer, the weather colder and colder. With a brave and lovely bright-ness in her eyes Mary took me to the boat. For the present we were defeated and I had to seek refuge at home.

II

Queenshaven was beautiful in its own type of wintry beauty. The sunlight filtered through the blue

air with a smooth, golden glow like honey. All objects
were defined with an indescribable clearness. The dry
spears of the palmettos rattled softly. My father and
mother were so glad to have me that, by tacit consent,
all troubling questions were dismissed. Also my
father's income had increased soemwhat and it seemed
to me that to be calm for a period and think hard was,
after all, the strictly practical thing to do. First of all,
it seemed clear to me then that I could not teach. Even
were it possible after long months or even years to get
a small appointment, I was unwilling to risk the sus-
pense and the humiliation. There was nothing left
me but such skill as I had in writing. But criticism
and verse would not suffice. Prose fiction was the only
thing at which one could earn a living. So I determined to become a short story writer and a novelist.
Perhaps I didn't reason the matter out quite so
coldly. Or else I let my reasoning be guided by a
strong and hitherto unsuspected impulse which stirred
somewhere in the depth of consciousness. The things
I had seen and lived through in New York with all the
impassioned observation and pain of youth seemed to
become denser at certain points, to gather—in my
imaginative memory—into definite motifs. I seemed
suddenly to be able to see them with a more penetrating eye. Fragments torn from the context of life
seemed to become organic, to lift themselves from the
more inert mass of experience and to take on an independent existence. What I needed next was a
method. I had never studied closely the technique of
modern fiction. A very sure instinct led me to Henry
James, to the clear, brimming stories of his middle
years: The Lesson of the Master, Broken Wings, The

Altar of the Dead. I soon knew what, for my purpose,
I needed to know. I didn't, I must say in justice to
myself, imitate Henry James at all. But no one with
the craftsman's insight can read these stories—I
lingered over about fifteen—without learning from
that close and scrupulous master the essential secrets
of imaginative narrative.

In a state of very high mental tension—extraordi-
narily clear and yet almost mystical—I wrote three
stories. Nothing I have ever done cost me so little
trouble. There was no change or erasure in the manuscripts. Yet I felt quite certain that the work had—
in structure, style, characterization—a real and a new
felicity. I am recording the feelings of the time; I
have not read the stories in years. But I was not
wholly wrong. For only a few months ago Dreiser
said to me: "Why don't you reprint those early
stories? I never saw stuff so full of a sense of beauty."

I typed my work and hesitated. A friend in New
York had once said thoughtfully: "Maybe you could
get stuff into the magazines more easily if you used a
pseudonym. Your name's very Jewish." I pondered
the matter. I did not know how absurd his notion was.
Should I use a pseudonym? Should I—it was possible
—make my name less foreign by a change in spelling?
I had a few difficult hours. Should I risk my last
chance? In spite of my recent experience I didn't feel
nearly so strongly on nationality and its rights in
America as I do now. Nevertheless I decided not to
betray myself even to the extent of concealing or of
altering my name. True, however, to the traditions
of my Queenshaven past, I sent my stories to the Atlantic Monthly.

In due time the editors of the Atlantic replied that "they were not unaware of the quality or significance of these sketches, but that even among the clientèle of the Atlantic there were, they feared, not enough people who would care for them." My mother and father, in their unalterable devotion to quality rather than profitableness of achievement, were proud of this evidently sincere statement. But I thought of Mary who was coming to visit my mother, and the fear crept over me that I might be doomed to penniless quality and unpopularity. It occurred to me that I knew nothing of the popular fiction of the day. So I tried to read stories in the magazines. But I couldn't. Nor have I succeeded since. The stuff pretends to render life and interpret it 'and has no contact with reality at any point. Dishonest, sapless twaddle, guided by an impossible moral perfectionism—a false perfectionism, too, since its ideals are always tribal—and strung on a string of pseudo-romantic love. I remembered, however, that I had once or twice read in the Smart Set stories with a touch, at least, of vitality, earnestness, verisimilitude. So I sent my rejected stories there. In less than two weeks came a letter from Charles Hanson Towne, who was then the editor. He accepted all three stories and asked for more.

III

One knows the kind of anecdote that is told of the literary aspirant. That's what he is called. The kind of advice—with its broad touch of commercialism and bourgeois canniness—that is given him. Never be discouraged! Rewrite! Send your stories in order to every magazine in the country! Watch what the editors want! Success to him who sticks it out—two years, three, five. Success—the current connotations of the word are enough to make a voluntary outcast of any self-respecting soul. Well, I said to myself, I had made up my mind four months before to write stories. The result showed the absurdity of the humdrum advice, the vulgar maxims of the tradesmen in letters. It did—in the deepest sense. Only I drew impossible inferences in the tense hopefulness of those days. And my delusion was fated to completeness. Joel Chandler Harris founded Uncle Remus' Magazine in Atlanta and bought my fourth story, sending, almost by return mail, a letter of enthusiastic praise and a checque for one hundred and twenty-five dollars. My father was, characteristically, aglow; he saw visions of grandeur. My mother's womanly and solitary heart yearned over Mary. So Mary and I were married and we all settled down in an old, roomy house in Queenshaven. The house overlooked the bay and from our study windows Mary and I watched the horned moon float over the silken swell of the dark waters and listened to the tide. . . .

Those altitudes of life are brief and have, upon retrospect, a touch of utter pathos. To be upon them you must, the world being what it is, be out of touch with reality. There is the temper, to be sure, that frankly accepts reality as sordid, mean, unresponsive to our finer impulses and, turning resolutely from it, strives after the illusions and takes refuge in the art that depicts life "as it ought to be." And commonly, in street and church and school among us, such people call themselves idealists and scorn us to whom the illu-

sion and the dream is too cheap a thing. To us there
comes, after the first flush of youth, the troubling sense
of being duped to no good or enduring purpose. We
come to live in an autumnal world of the spirit. . . .
Yet we are the true lovers of the ideal. We refuse to
be put off with a wretched substitute. Either the values
by which we would live are valid in the world of reality
or they are not. If they are not, it is better and wiser
to know and to submit. The eternal children among
men, on the other hand, pass from toy to toy. Yet in
the end they must see—with what a late and grey and
piteous disillusion—that their toys are but tinsel and
wax and bran. . . .

Mary and I believed that here, in our American
place and time, fine, sound, veracious art would easily
gain for us the wherewithal for our very frugal needs
and joys. I wrought out my stories with the severest
exactions upon structure, verbal grace, inner truth.
Towne bought more of them. The editor of a weekly
of rather shady reputation asked for stories. A sense
of insecurity which gradually overcame me persuaded
me to sell him my manuscripts. If the stories were as
perfect as I could make them, what did it matter? Unhappily all these people paid only a cent a word. I
spent two weeks of the most highly organized artistic
labor over a story and the material result was thirty
dollars—payable at some hazy date months ahead. I
summoned my deepest and serenest powers and wrote
a longer narrative and sent it to Harper's. Henry
Mills Alden saw its artistic points and half agreed to
buy it—if I would give it a happy ending. But the
story didn't end happily! I looked at Mary. She
should have had a new gown. And so, for the first

time, I went in for the trade of writing and altered the ending of my story. But Alden didn't take the story, after all.

A happy ending. Cheerfulness. Here are the rocks on which I suffered my second ship-wreck in life. For the Alden incident is merely the type and symbol of many others. All the editors admitted that my stories had very uncommon merits. But they were too sombre. . . . Once, just once, I wrote a story full of gentle pathos. With a touch of irony I called it A Sentimental Story. When it appeared editors from all quarters wrote to me. Send us stories like your Sentimental Story! The abysmal folly! I could no more recapture that mood—so unlike my typical moods—than I could bring back the perished hour in which that mood had come to me. Of such considerations, as of the whole nature of art, the editors seemed to be densely ignorant.

I determined to make myself independent of the magazines and their absurd requirements. I felt the need of a larger canvas anyhow. So, writing just stories enough for our barest needs—my father and mother kept the pot boiling and paid the rent—I began a novel.

My subject wasn't, I can see now, a highly fruit-ful one. Nor had I yet quite transcended the notion that one must follow to some definite end in circumstances the strands of the narrative. In other words, I was still unaware of the endless flowing of the world, of the utter absence of finality at any point except the point of death. And also, a subtle and troubled sense of what—through the editors and through personal talk—I suspected concerning the attitude of my American audience, prevented me, at many points, from practising my art in its full severity. One must have bread. . . . Yet, with every allowance made, the thing was felt, seen, rendered. It was young, that first novel of mine, but there were pages and chapters that both in the texture of the prose and the shaping of the matter had a touch of life and beauty.

Often now I wrote on my sheer nerves. A sense of discouragement had come over us all. Small checques for stories dribbled in from time to time. But my father had to work harder than ever. Instead of lifting the burden of life from him and my mother I had, in the material sense, added to it. The thing was unendurable and throbbed in me with the fierceness of a wound. Then the manuscript of my novel came back from a large publishing house, and in the smiting heat of the Queenshaven summer Mary fell ill.

With a sense, at last, almost of despair, my father and I borrowed some money. I had to get another start, to lift the burden from him, to fight my own man's battle. My mother and I had a sense of the bitter tragedy of that parting, though we sought to conceal it even from ourselves and though Mary was full of cheer and sweetness and courage. Ferris rose to the occasion and came to the train to see us off. Perhaps he had a suspicion of how broken and defeated I felt.

IV

We took a small flat on Washington Heights. The house was new, but it was dingy by nature—cheap, ugly, abominable. Yet we had the Hudson landscape almost at our door and we had money enough for three months and the Smart Set owed me a checque or two. So Mary and I picnicked in our little kitchen—we had no dining-table—and felt more hopeful. And there was a glow in our shabby study when Towne sent an enthusiastic letter concerning the manuscript of the novel and promised to get a publisher for it.

Meantime I had to make money. The respectable magazines would have none of me. They rejected my poems and stories with rigid regularity. The editors never failed to praise my work and never dreamed of buying it. There was something in it—on that point they were unanimous and clear—which their subscribers would not endure. Towne, my one editorial friend, introduced me to the editor-in-chief of the Munsey magazines, an agreeable, sweet-natured Irishman. The latter and his assistant, always hard pressed for copy, gave a little luncheon party for me and explained to me the mysteries of the "serial." The All-Story Magazine, The Scrap-Book, The Cavalier, were in constant need of serial stories of from twenty thousand to sixty thousand words in length. These serials had to be built in blocks of three chapters, each block thus constituting a ten thousand word installment. Each chapter had to end with a minor device of suspended mystery, each installment with a major device. The mystery must not be solved until the last chapter of the last installment. Nor must it be solved then by any method involving an explanatory or retrospective narrative. There must be little description and no analysis. There must be a powerful love interest but no hint of sex. The pay for these marvelous concoctions was two-thirds of a cent a word. But the bait for the struggling hack lay in this.

You could drivel to the tune of sixty thousand words and the company paid on acceptance. I am glad to record this significant little feature of our civilization. No one else is likely to do it. And these magazines sold enormously at that time.

They had given me some excellent wine at the luncheon party and as I walked up-town on the Avenue the proposal seemed an admirable one with which to bridge over the time until the novel should make my fame and fortune. At home I took a soberer view. I hadn't a particle of ingenuity; I had trained myself in the austerest methods of the novelist's art. Flaubert, James, Conrad were my teachers. Above all, George Moore. I wrote slowly, with infinite pains, weighing each word for its values in flavor, color, tone—hovering over the melody of the sentence, the harmony of the paragraph, desperate when the beauty of the prose failed to orchestrate the strain of the meaning. . . . But I had to make money.

I thought closely: There was no earthly way of building a Munsey serial except upon a motif of pursuit. And it must be the pursuit of a criminal, a treasure or a girl. Preferably of two—the criminal is responsible for his original crime plus the disappearance of the girl. Or a pursuit of all three—the criminal's crime involves spiriting away the treasure and the girl. Then, in the last chapter of the last installment the hero defeats the criminal, obtains the treasure, marries the girl. So far the thing worked out with mathematical accuracy. Each yarn must then be individualized by differences in setting and incident and such touches of quaintness or breadth of adventurousness as could be given it. I reread Henry Esmond and The Master of Balantrae for that note of gallant spiritedness which is common to both. Then, from the half-forgotten narratives of a Queenshaven acquaintance—a seaman turned shoe-merchant—I built up my first synopsis. This synopsis was pronounced good by the editors and I proceeded to the task of composition. Now came the rub. I had to get rid of my usual style and point of view. They were worse than useless for the purpose. I had to write briskly and in a falsetto. I struggled for days. Then came the solution. I ceased composing with pen and paper. On the typewriter I could assume the whole alien outlook and tone and turn out, on good days, copy adequate for the purpose without change or erasure. I have written as high as six thousand words of serial stuff a day, driving my Gibson hero over land and sea, by hair-breadth 'scapes, until he had the villain (usually, by a pleasant American convention, a foreigner) by the throat and a girl and a treasure in each arm.

I wrote and sold six serials against every human and artistic instinct of my nature. Then I broke down. The vein of base invention wouldn't yield another drop; the insufferable falseness of the whole business literally turned my stomach. I was ready to do anything, suffer anything—only not write serials.

∇

Meanwhile there was the novel, the thought of which sustained Mary and me. Towne had given it to Dreiser and Dreiser liked it. We had been reading Sister Carrie which had just made its second and definite appearance, and Dreiser's approval repaid me amply for the snubs of the commercial editors and publishers. True that Dreiser had no style. Neither had Balzac. And yet even those quaint vulgarities of phrase, which he has since eliminated, helped to render his subject in Sister Carrie. Occasionally, too, through the sheer fullness and exactness of that penetrating vision of his he strikes out curious, unlovely, journalese little sentences that are worth tons of ordinary smooth writing. And how he wrings and cleanses the heart with the fates of his people! There is no profounder illustration than the character of Hurstwood in all literature of the great saying of Goethe that every concrete thing, if it perfectly represents itself, becomes the sufficient symbol of all. We know this man as we know few men in life. And we know, too, if we can begin to feel the approach of middle age, that there is a Hurstwood in each one of us. . . .

I went to see Dreiser and felt less shame over my serials. For wasn't he editing The Delineator? The old question of bread. His office high up in the Butterick building had from its large windows one of the most splendid and heroic views in the world—far across the harbor of New York. There he sat, a large, unshapely, sombre hulk of a man—(he has brightened and softened since)—with head bent forward, folding and eternally unfolding his handkerchief into accordion pleats. There was a brooding gaze in his nearsighted eyes—the gaze with which he has seen life more largely and truly than any other American novelist. And he has let life interpret itself upon the basis of its eternal facts. He has let life mean—life! Not some moralistic crochet that is the weapon of his own intolerance. By virtue of that quality he is, in his humble and homespun way, of the kin, at least, of the masters. Of what did Homer approve, or Shakespeare, or Rembrandt or Goethe?

Dreiser recommended my novel to the small firm of publishers who had recently brought out Sister Carrie. So, very soon, I had my first contract in my pocket and was very proud of it, and Mary and I walked on a memorable night under a huge, pale moon on Wadsworth Avenue and reckoned out how much we would have if our novel—we called it ours—sold twenty thousand copies. If it sold only ten thousand—? Oh, it would be a beginning, and I could write another in peace and there would be no more serials. I sent an enthusiastic letter to my mother and father and they trusted as we did.

The novel appeared. For a first book the critical reception was remarkable. William Morton Payne wrote of it in a well-known journal as a book "in which the imperative demands of technique—both verbal and architectonic—are never ignored, and which yet has no lack of rich human substance. . . . It is not a book for the young person to read," he went on, "but one from which the mature mind can get nothing but good and which offers a singular satisfaction to the artistic perceptions." Similar was the tone of other reviews. There was generous praise, to be sure, but never without some subtle implication of warning. A mythical, at least, a theoretical "young person" was, somehow, to be guarded against my book. A number of reviewers took up the cudgels for this young person and belabored me in unmeasured terms. The Presbyterian editor of the Queenshaven Courier, a friend of mine— (I thought)—arose in his wrath and his terror for the young person and abused my book in terms that were literally foul-mouthed. . . . An old college friend from Queenshaven asked me, months later, what my wife thought of the book. He asked it with the leer of free-masonry in nastiness which moral men assume in smoking-rooms. To him there was no difference between a smutty joke and a naturalistic novel. He would have read Mme. Bovary in secret, as a "dirty book," and hidden it from his wife. To her who was "sweet and pure" he gives, I know, the works of Robert Chambers and Harold Bell Wright. . . . I reflected on the young person for whom American literature is kept "clean and wholesome." How old was this young person? Evidently seventeen, at least. For the most foolish parent would supervise the reading of youngsters under that age without necessarily condemning the books withheld. And was the young American at seventeen such an imbecile that the central passions of life—their existence even—if presented and interpreted in art came in the nature of a revelation? Or else so vicious that true books would start him straightway on an abandoned career? Surely not! Then it was but again the old, ineradicable lust for lying, for unveracity of soul, for an unfeatured and unmeaning harmlessness of surface—the old duality of conscience which makes men pretend that the thing is what it is not, but rather some foolish, blank, marrowless phantom. . . . Literature, to be wholesome, my friend the professor of English philology used to tell me, should portray life as it ought to be. How ought it to be? Ah, cheerful, sober, kindly . . . like the Book of Job, I suppose, or the Illiad, or the Divine Comedy or Lear or Faust! Without passion or sorrow or the hardihood of thought. . . . Base-ball, prohibition and the Saturday Evening Post. What spiritual implications of a national culture.

How could my poor little book, brave such an array of forces? It didn't sell. It didn't sell at all. I wrote another without one touch of the sensuous beauty of the first—a bare, plain, austere transcript from life, holding within itself, because it is of the very core of realty, a massive moral implication. This book, of which I am still proud in retrospect, was published too. And Anthony Comstock, that human symbol of the basic lies of our social structure, confiscated the copies and caused the plates to be destroyed. I was beaten, broken, breadless. I was a scholar and forbidden to teach, an artist and forbidden to write. Liberty, opportunity. The words had nothing friendly to my ear.

VI

Mary and I agreed that, so defeated, we couldn't go home both for our own and for my parents' sake. It would be only a palliative, after all. Somehow, though all the forces of life seemed against me—my health was poor now, too—I must struggle on. And so there comes to me now from that period the memory of many months, strangely quiet, for all the care and need, and full of an almost eerie sunshine. I see Mary and myself wandering across queer neighborhoods—a sticky, swarming yet faintly genteel street called Bradhurst Avenue—on our way to Third. Somewhere about us we carried, carefully wrapped, the silver spoons we were going to pawn. The gas-bill had to be paid or the milk-bill. Then my father, in his ever watchful goodness, would send a money-order or a small checque would come in and we would take a long tramp just for fun. Up Riverside Drive to Dyckman Street or into queer neighborhoods in the Bronx where we discovered, among many other things, an empty, sandy, forlorn little street called Shakespeare Avenue. These wanderings rested my worn nerves.

I am not quite sure how we did live. My father helped. Friends helped—friends of Mary and of mine, now of us both—friends who had and have no motive but their affection for us, our friends still, Jew and Gentile, of whom it touches me to think. I wrote reviews for The Nation and The Forum. I read manuscripts for a friendly publishing house. I gave a few private lessons. But the situation was an impossible one. It was only putting off week by week—how often we did pawn the silver—a day of inevitable collapse.

I went back to Brent. It was a bitter thing to be forced to do. He set in motion the whole machinery of the department, he gave me the full weight of his influence. It was useless. I was refused at the University of Virginia—because I was a Jew. I was refused at the University of Minnesota—because I was a Jew. The reason was scarcely veiled; it was not debatable. Ellard was now teaching at Monroe. He plead with his chief and Brent and Richards wrote to the man. He refused me—because I was a Jew. . . . Brent felt, rightly, that he was at the end of his resources. No one could have done more.

It occurred to me, of course, that I might teach German. But I felt, in a sense, insufficiently prepared. My philological training, for instance, had all been from the point of view of English. But Richards, like

Brent, had faith in me and brushed that consideration aside. An instructorship at Princeton was vacant. Richards showed me the letter which he wrote to the head of the German Department there. He spoke of my abilities, of my character, of my personality. He touched on the fact of my race and defended me with noble emphasis from its supposed or real faults. I was refused. . . . Some years later a university in the farther West needed a professor of German. The attention of the Dean there was called to my work and reputation as a scholar and teacher. He wrote me a tentative letter. I answered but never heard again. Later he confided to a friend of mine that he had sounded the trustees. It would have been useless to propose the name of a Jew. . . . All the men who had refused me at the various universities were Anglo-Americans, pillars of the democracy, proclaimers of its mission to set the bond free and equalize life's opportunities for mankind. I shall be accused, of course, of making too much of this matter. Not so. I may not be borne out by To-day. But there will be a To-morrow. It was a legitimate and searching test of the democratic pretensions of the society which these men represent and of the temper of that society. Their reactions register accurately the spirit of the nativistic oligarchy which rules us. . . . By this time Ellard was thoroughly alarmed for me. He went to his friend, the head of the German Department at Monroe and laid the matter before him. Ellard's friend—now for years mine too,—is a German, the finest, deepest-souled type. In six weeks I had my appointment to an instructorship at Monroe. . . .

The months between April and October had to be

bridged. But I got a piece of translation to do and also, refreshed by hope for the future, I wrote one more serial. In my leisure hours I wrote a text-book in the field of Germanics so as to make a respectable entrance into my new profession. I meant to devote myself undividedly to it, for I was convinced now, through experience and reflection, that my art product could not, in this age, commend itself to the strange minds of my countrymen. To poetry only did I hope to devote some time in the future. But I was not aware of all the conditions within the academic life, nor did I count with the heaviness of the coming years.

I had not been at home in many months. Mary was kept in New York by a misfortune among her kin. So I went alone with a feeling, half of delight and half of bitter, grinding remorse. I had a job. But I was twenty-eight and the job paid one thousand dollars a year. I had wanted to do so much. I came with empty hands. I had seen the color of life now and was able to estimate my chances. And so I knew that the good dream of the years was over and that I would never lift my father and mother out of the life they were living, that I would not even be able ever to dwell near them again, but always half a continent away. Final and fatal issues. At home they did not make these thoughts hard for me, God knows, but were glad in the bit of luck that had come and my mother promised to visit Mary and me in the West and so make the long year of absence shorter. I stayed at home ten weeks, happy weeks, though often I felt a tremor of unearthly fear—all the old eerie dread for my mother. . . .

And in the quietude of my own mind I went over the years that had gone by since I had first left home.

I went over these years bit by bit. What were their fruits? In every worldly sense—not only in the base one—I had been and I was a wretched failure. Yet I could not help believing that I had good, even notable talents. I knew also that sloth or shirking were not among my faults of mind or character. Why, then had it been so? It had been so, the answer came, because a man can make neither his gifts nor his character count except through those methods and institutions which society has organized. From these I had hitherto been, in many subtle ways and in one way that was gross and obvious, mercilessly excluded.

I had turned to creative art. But my stories and novels had failed, because my way of looking at life seemed strange and sinister to most of my countrymen. For my vision of it was not of a superficial, kindly affair, all pleasantly prearranged. "If you do so, you are good and happy, if otherwise, bad and unhappy, and, what is worse, not like what other folks desire to think they are." . . . For the last time I read the successful novels of that year. That way were fame and fortune. But the stuff made me feel doubly hopeless and doubly innocent. The stories were cheerful—like cheerful liars. They were not about harsh things or noble things like myrrh or wine, only about doleful things and sweetish things, like soup and liquorice. They were not about love and aspiration and death. They were about flirting and success and old folks' homes. They were not even pure, they were only proper. Life, in them, wasn't even austere, only expurgated. They were false to the shallow core of them, false and dishonorable. The period, it is to be remembered, was 1910. But even today an eminent artist like Sherwood Anderson finds the conventional periodicals inaccessible and suffers the obvious consequences.

Once more then, I accepted my fate. But it was not easy. For the weeks rolled by and I knew that I was going a thousand miles away and had no idea when I would be able to earn money enough to come back. Not for myself did my resignation to rigorous poverty cut into my soul, nor for Mary—for she and I had each other and friends and the years to come—but for the sake of those two wan faces that disappeared from my sight as the train pulled out of the Queenshaven station.

CHAPTER VII

THE BUSINESS OF EDUCATION.

I

Monroe is a forest city set among lakes. Indian burial mounds dot the hills and beside one of those blue lakes shy tepees appear overnight at certain seasons. The air is sharp, tonic and primitive. The storms of autumn sweep through the great trees with a severe and iron music. City and lakes and forests have in my memory an air that is primaeval and yet somehow touched with grace and learning. They seem as established as a temple, yet as wild as an eagle's wing. The university is set upon a hill; its walls and groves are mirrored in the most beautiful of the five lakes. For years Monroe and its memories had to suffice me for my inner springs of beauty. To-day that beauty, like so much else in the world, is scarred and tarnished in my mind. . . .

Mary was kept in the East by illness among her people. I came alone to Monroe during the sparkle and glow of its Indian summer. Ellard met me and we passed some weeks in talking and rowing near the yellow and bronze and scarlet of the lake shores. With a fine sagacity that I have always found in the most poetical spirits—not in mere artistic temperaments—

he gave me pithy and exact advice in regard to this
new career and activity and in regard to the char-
acters of the men with whom I was to live and work.
He took me to see my chief Vollberg—tall, elegant,
careworn, expansive, one of the soundest minds and
hearts in the world; to B., all burning eyes, domed
forehead, Socratic nose, sputtering, lyrical speech,
afterwards my special friend and comrade of that
group; to F., accomplished, handsome, but too good a
lover of beauty to be worldly in an evil sense; to P.,
with his snapping, black Slavic eyes and snapping,
ironic speech and vast learning. And these were only
a few of that astonishing German department which
was, in my time, one of the goodliest fellowships of
comradely and learned men on earth. Most of them are
gone from there now—scattered and futile and alone.
They think of Monroe, I am sure, and B., at least, who
is still there, remembers that first departmental jaunt
in which I took part—miles of autumnal forest and
golden field and then an inn, and free and racy talk
on art and life and scholarship; supper of roast fowl
and potatoes and cool, yellow beer, and then the walk
back over the shivering tracery of the trees' shadows
on the long, moonlit road. Such memories are precious amid the waste and confusion of later years. They
ring and gleam across time from a saner and serener
world. . . .

The sense of both liberation and security which my
first academic position gave me, the beauty of Monroe,
the presence of Ellard, the forming of new friendships
—all these things caused me to take immediately a
very glowing view of my situation. Moreover, the
University of Monroe was at that time at the highest

point of its effectiveness and power. It had been neither crippled by legislative interference nor darkened and distraught by war; it was as nearly as possible the free seat of learning of a strong and hopeful democracy. Hence I felt something of a freedom and a power that I had sought elsewhere in vain. What helped me in addition was that, from the first, I proved to be a very successful teacher. It is worth while dwelling for a moment on this fact. If I have harsh things to say of our whirring educational machine, they do not spring from the uneasiness of personal irritation. From that first fall in Monroe to the end of my academic career eight years later, I had in the fullest measure possible among us, the reward that makes a teacher's life endurable—the loyalty and the gratitude of my students. I exacted of them always their best work and straightest thinking; I tolerated no cheap phrases or tribal formularies in my class-room. Hence my colleagues soon thought me a little more showy than safe. The students never failed me—in Monroe or Central City, in peace or war.

Why did I leave Monroe? Vollberg begged me to stay. Ellard, in the grip of an intimate tragedy, needed me. The Dean was persuasive. Well, certain responsibilities, which shall be nameless, had to be faced and every penny was important. I had been so happy in Monroe that a strong instinct in me rebelled against making it the scene of penury, grime and chagrin. Also, a wild restlessness often came over me when I remembered the more than thousand miles that stretched between my mother and myself. My old life in which I was so deeply rooted, my own past and my family's, which I had come to see with a

new warmth and sympathy and compassion—all that
seemed terribly far away and almost blotted out here.
Thus an acute peacelessness stirred always at the
core of me. At all events, when a friend in the department was called to the chairmanship of the department in Central City and asked me to go with him,
I accepted the offer, though not without doubt and
hesitation.

Mary and I raised money somehow, went for a few
brief weeks to Queenshaven and came to Central City
to establish ourselves. That establishment was slow
and difficult and never complete. We had both been
accustomed to richer and racier forms of life than we
found in that characteristic city of the Middle West, to
a more flexible society, a freer air. But we were de-
stined to stay there for six years. It was there that I
watched the color of life and brooded upon death and
war and felt the pang of youth leaving my heart; there
I wrote several books that brought me some small re-
pute and sat in final judgment on my poetry. There,
too, I thought at one time that I had learned the lesson of resignation. . . .

II

I applied myself to the business of education. To
what we, in America, call the higher education of the
most democratic type. For the university of Central
City is a state institution. It is coeducational. There
are between five and six thousand students and a faculty of nearly five hundred. The university is divided
into eight chief colleges to all but one of which—the
college of medicine—a graduation certificate from a

high school admits the student. In a word, any **boy or** girl in the state who has completed a high school course may go to Central City and learn anything within the whole realm of human knowledge which may seem most effective in developing the individual. These state universities represent a handsome ideal. If the teaching were not propaganda, if the teachers were not slaves. . . . Yet from these universities fiery things may one day come. Not now. Let me remember. . . .

I stroll on the campus in spring as I have done many times. The students are not disturbed by my approach, for they stand in no particular awe of their professors. Those that know me go on with their conversation, simply including me in it if I stop. They know that my attitude is always comradely. I watch their faces. There is not a vicious face on the campus. I try to recall one among the hundreds of students I have taught. I cannot. Dull faces, vacant faces. Not one that expresses any corruption of heart and mind. I look about me again and watch for one face that betrays a troubled soul, a yearning of the mind, the touch of any flame. There is none. How many such faces have I seen in class-room or campus? I count them: one, two, three—well, four. I must except the handful of Russian Jews. Thought and emotion are their birthright. But my young Americans? Many of the girls are dainty and comely. The peasant is obliterated here in a single generation. The boys have bright and cheery faces—rather more flattened and less salient, upon the whole, than the girls'. A little coarser in modelling and tinting. But all, all incurably trivial. I listen to their talk. It is of games, parties, examinations. Never of the contents of the tests. But of the practical fact that they have to be faced. Who has ever heard an eager argument among these students on any of the subjects—art, religion, economics, sex—that are supposed to employ the minds of men? Who has ever seen them keen about anything except (symbolically speaking) football and fudge? It is, as a matter of fact, considered rather bad form among them to show any stirring of the mind. It is considered "high-brow," queer, that is to say—different, personal and hence, by a subtle and quite mad implication consoling to stupidity and emptiness—undemocratic.

A Continental would ask: Why do they go to the university? In Central City comparatively few went for social reasons. An extraordinary proportion of the students earn their maintenance wholly or in part. They and their parents make real sacrifices in the cause of education. I found few of those young men and women really slack and trifling. There was practically no disciplinary problem. The students came to the class-room to learn something. I have seen both French and German friends speechless before that contradiction. But gradually I fought my way to its true meaning which is this: To the "average, intelligent American" education, for which he is willing to deny himself and pay taxes, means—skill, information—at most, accomplishment. Skill and knowledge with which to conquer the world of matter. It does not mean to him an inner change—the putting on of a new man, a new criterion of truth, new tastes and other values. The things he wants at the university are finer and more flexible tools for the economic war which he calls liberty. And like tools or weapons they are external to him and are dropped when the class-room period or the working day are over. He then merges himself again into the great level of the democratic mass from which he strives to be distinguished only by the possession of those sharper tools. By his outlook upon life, his distinction of taste, his finer palate for truth he would hesitate to be differentiated from his fellows. He would seem to himself in danger of being a "high-brow" and a snob. Occasionally I used to hear a gifted student, alive to the deeper meaning of the humanities, passionately disclaim the values he had himself attained in a blind terror of non-conformity. And I heard students say, not once or twice: "But the majority is of another opinion; I'm probably wrong." And why not? There was the President of the university in Central City who led the way.

The man has been on my mind all these years. And the other day I made a record of him and of his meaning.

* * * * * * * *

During a recent crisis of our national history a certain distinguished citizen of my acquaintance— college president, insurance magnate, farmer, and merchant—announced with an indescribable unction: "My opinion is that of the average American." His broad lips tightened and his eyes became stony. He turned up his sleeves, figuratively speaking, to enforce his own loyalty upon all within his power. For loyalty is what he called it and had always called it. He had been loyal to his college and to his college-team, to his party—the Republican—his state, his city and his church. He had always acted from within a group and had always identified himself with that group's opinion of itself and with its attitude to other groups. The qualities of these other groups he had always loyally excluded from his experience. He had never permitted himself really to see the rival team, the competing institution, or the other party. No wonder then that he swept aside with a muscular gesture a suggestion that he should, in this supreme moment, envisage humanity as at least including the alien and hostile tribe. Once somebody asked him: "Then you interpret loyalty to a social group—college, church, city, nation—as an identification of one's own opinion with the majority opinion held within that group at the quite arbitrary moment when the group chooses to apply a test?" He became truculent and oratorical. The question had simply not reached his mind. His very conception of loyalty had involved the submersion of his reason. He was impenetrable.

And yet to my own knowledge, in the ordinary, concrete matters of daily living this man was both wise and just. The old experiences of the race that had recurred within his own life he had grasped firmly, and concerning these his judgment was liberal and ripe. He had been poor in his earlier years and his underpaid colleagues found him to be both understanding and helpful; he had been married several times and had a saner insight than many supposed into the intricate relations of men and women. He had, in all such matters, an occasional bluntness of speech that proved him to be free from the grosser delusions of his fellows. Wherever his personal experience guided his judgment, that judgment was sound. On all other matters he talked like a child or a madman and, at critical moments, fell back upon the mass judgment of men whose opportunities for experience were even more restricted than his own. This process he called "loyalty" and it gave him the mien and temper of an inquisitor. In his personal life he experienced and reasoned from experience; the motives of his political actions were savage and confused.

It seems to me that this man's character is a symbol. Judgments formed without experience are vain and in the void. But mankind has evidently not the power of transmitting experiences that do not repeat themselves within the actual life of each generation. The simplest know that fire burns and snow chills and even that thrift makes for order. But so soon as intervals elapse between experiences they are either obliterated or transformed into romance. The ages pass and war follows war. Mankind has not learned that the blow returned does not heal the pain of the blow suffered, neither does it touch the impulse that aimed the blow, nor cure the suffering from which that impulse leaped, nor make order of the moral chaos in which the suffering was born. It follows that all judgments in regard to war and peace, all corporate or collective judgments in moments of crisis and on matters that have not been constant factors in the lives of the individuals who compose the group are wholly and necessarily worthless. You may call an acquiescence in such judgments by ringing names—teamwork, loyalty, patriotism. It remains a savage thing and the chief enemy in our path.

What are we to do? Have not even historians, warders of the rarer experiences of the race, failed us at crises? The answer lies here, so at least it seems to me; we can not change the nature of man, but we can affect his mood. Christianity did that for some centuries, the ideal of economic co-operation does so to-day. We can attack the concept of loyalty as excluding inquiry and experience; we can seek to merge the mind's freedom with its own self-respect. We can begin humbly. When the leader of the school foot-ball team announces certain victory based on nothing but his craving to show the superiority of his particular group, his teachers can explain the spiritual vulgarity of that impulse, insist on an imaginative grasp of the rival team's likeness to his own and thus temper the ferocity of the merely competitive instincts. We can deprecate all forms of "booming" and "boosting"; we can point out a humility which is also a nobler form of pride. We can substitute a sense of personal and inner worth for the misery and emptiness that fling the individual into blind group-action to satisfy his primitive will to superiority and power. We can show that judgment without experience will wreck a society as surely as it will wreck an individual, and that loyalty to the humblest truth a man has found for himself is better than to cheer whole acres of bunting or to wear a gaudy ribbon in his coat.

* * * * * * * *

Our students, then, came to the university not to find truth, but to be engineers or farmers, doctors or teachers. They did not want to be different men and women. It is in conformity with this popular purpose that the elective system of studies has been pushed back from the college into the high-school and that state universities have been compelled, by actual legislation is some cases, to admit high-school graduates simply by virtue of a definite amount of study without distinction of content or quality. The recent introduction of psychological tests when it is not, as in certain private universities of the East, a weapon against radicals and Jews, can be made to function in precisely the same way. And I do not say that, given the aim, the system is not practical. If the aim of education is merely to gain rough, useful tools for striving with the world of matter, and to gain them rapidly—the system works. I suppose that these state universities do turn out very fair engineers and farmers and veterinarians. But when their job leaves these men free they are but little different from people who have not gone to college. They go to foolish plays, read silly magazines and fight for every poisonous fallacy in politics, religion and conduct. A professor of geology in the university of Central City was publicly converted by Billy Sunday. The fact that he was not thereupon privately "fired," that he was still thought capable of teaching his science, symbolized the situation in its naked horror.

III

One or two of my colleagues and I were wont, in our interpretation of literature and thought, to speak freely in the class-room of those deep and serious matters concerning which it befits men and women to think all their lives. A few students—a very few—followed our leading. A number, also small, offered a sullen resistance. The majority considered us interesting, stimulating, a little quaint, and regarded these lectures as pleasant exercitations which had no contact with reality. A student, for example, would take advanced courses in philosophy and literature and return, with no sense of discrepancy, to the formularies of a third-rate conventicle. Another, a girl with a face full of intelligence and vivid sweetness, "majored" in French literature. She knew the language well and had read widely. But Montaigne and Anatole France never spoke to her. Her real interest was in Y. W. C. A. work and she was anxious to become a missionary. Her one desire was to save the followers of Buddha through the doctrines of the Fifth Street Baptist Church.

This phenomenon was a recurrent one. So let me repeat: Our people do not believe in education at all—if education means a liberation of the mind or a heightened consciousness of the historic culture of mankind. Philosophy and morals are taken care of by the Fifth Street Baptist Church. College is to fit you to do things—build bridges, cure diseases, teach French. It is not supposed to help you to be.

Convictions on all ultimate questions our students brought with them ready-made or continued deliberately to draw from sources other than ourselves. And these convictions constitute the most rigid and the palest inner culture by which, I suppose, any society has ever tried to live. I wonder whether I can describe this inner culture objectively. I know it almost tangibly. For years I read it in the eyes of my students, noted it in all their reactions, bruised myself daily against its dull and vicious edges. If I understood this ethos rightly, it holds that the aim and end of life is happiness in terms of blameless prosperity. It very sincerely distrusts intensity or distinction of mind and carelessness of material success. These things make for error and do not make for prosperity. It does not believe in virtue—*virtus,* power, the creative instinct in the intellectual or moral world—but wholly in such negative commandments as will contribute to honest material well-being. You must not drink fermented liquors, you must not criticize your neighbor harshly, you must not—except in business where the contrary is the supreme law—act selfishly; you must not doubt that America has achieved an unexampled freedom nor that the majority is right—"they say: 'the majority rules' "—and hence you must shun non-conformity to the fundamental beliefs of the majority as undemocratic and un-American. Also as un-Christian. For the Churches have substituted prohibition for saintliness and a state of economic competition in which blamelessness achieves prosperity for the kingdom of God.

How, it will be asked, can such convictions—so hum-drum, so middle-aged, so unheroic—armor as with steel the impassioned spirit of youth? Alas, youth in Central City had no rebellions or curiosities or yearnings. Young things there were not wild things. Adolescents neither wrote verse nor broke idols. A thoughtful physician assured me that nine-tenths of those young Americans with their untroubled eyes and steady gaze were undersexed. And I found a weighty confirmation in this: it was practically impossible, in studying literature, to get an emotional response. Those students had no emotional experience. Their inner lives were supremely poverty-stricken. Nothing in them cried out. In addition, their morality is one of restraint and negation. So that whatever feeble sparks of personality might smoulder here and there are smothered by the morals and beliefs of the mass-life. Thus personality itself came to seem almost wicked and propriety synonymous with goodness. If they could live so quietly in a moral world which seemed to have no contact with reality, it was because reality in them had little sharpness or insistence. They had become what home and church and school wanted them to be. The ideal of conformity, of colorlessness, of taking the world to be a tame and shop-keeping sort of affair had been achieved. . . .

Democracy was—was it not?—to set the individual free, to make room in the world for all types of personality, to make life comradely, vivid, flexible? My students had one positive instinct. It was quiet and it never became cruel. But it was unbreakable: the instinct of intolerance. They were quietly intolerant of all qualitative distinctions—even in themselves. I said to a class of seniors: "High-brow is usually a term applied by ignorant people to those whose finer qualities and insights they should seek to emulate." My class laughed in its pleasant, courteous way. An hour later in the library I witnessed this scene. A blond, tousle-headed lad, my chief comfort during a certain year, was trying to sell copies of a magazine which, with the help of the Russian Jewish students, he had tentatively established. The magazine was crude enough. But it was alive. There was verse in it, unrhythmed and gawky, but hopeful, and prose with some close thinking in it and a social outlook and a breath of the future. My friend Jim smiled at me and shouted: "Buy the second number of The Torch!" One of my seniors passed, the daughter of a federal judge. She shook her smooth, comely head with a self-satisfied little grin: "Too high-brow for me!" There was an inimitably characteristic little upward inflection on the last word. She bought The Sly-Cat—the students' comic paper—you may be sure, and laughed over its unspeakable inanities. It was natural, you say. The act—yes. But the spirit of the act! She refused The Torch with self-righteous triumph and read The Sly-Cat with a solid sense of doing the right thing—because it was the ordinary thing. She had made a fetish of commonness—except in the matter of money and clothes and motor-cars. So had they all. . . .

IV

If they had met a solid front when they came to Central City, had met detachment, resistance, the critical and distinguishing mind! But the university caters to the High Schools and these to the grade schools and the grade schools to what the hardware-man and the undertaker think their Johns and Wesleys and Ruths and Helens ought to learn. Here is the incurable dilemma of democracy. A democratic community, in order to be free, wise, self-governed, needs minds that are so—minds that will think closely, resist delusions, discriminate and really will and choose. An historic and philosophic culture is, in a democracy, no longer a luxury or an accomplishment. It is a bitter necessity. Lacking it, the group-life is at the mercy of every odious folly, of every brazen demagogue, of every machine-boss, of every catch-word. . . . But how shall we persuade our masters, the hardwareman and the undertaker, that what John and Wesley need for good citizenship, for honest citizenship, in the plain and literal sense, is not more skill, but history, philosophy, economics, literature—a spiritual background, a sense of values, a vision of man's life, of "Florence, Weimar, Athens, Rome?" It can not be done. The sage can be disinterested and so can the proletarian. The undertaker and the hardwareman. striving always to be managers of a casket trust or a plow share monopoly, are hopelessly committed to the economic and intellectual *status quo*. Hence a bourgeois democracy is rigid. This is its dilemma. Whoever possesses or hopes to possess more than he needs, more than a house, a garden, a room full of books, is doomed to keeping static the order in which he lives.

Well, in our present system of education the decrees of the hardwareman and the undertaker have been carried out. Thus, in Central City, there are charming buildings for the school of veterinary medicine, handsome and commodious ones for agriculture and engineering, domestic science, chemistry and forestry. The ancient arts and studies of man that give vision and wisdom are squeezed in somehow. The students see all that and it falls in with the notions they already have of what is useful and what is not. They tolerate the required Freshman English because of a dim something connected with business letters and advertising "dope." Their spoken English remains, as a matter of fact, hopelessly corrupt. They used to elect German because a "lot of science is written in German." The war rather eased them of that discipline. Spanish, more recently, is chosen on account of a vague notion about the South American trade. The proof of the reality of these motives is that in Central City there was never more than one small section of Italian. No science there that they know of, no business either. The advanced courses in language and literature, including English, are filled with girls who can afford the agreeable and the useless. Greek is dead. Latin is still studied by a handful of young women who teach it in High School because "there's so much Latin in English and so many scientific terms are Latin." The reason of spiritual poltroonry. In another generation the classics of the English tongue will be as obsolete as a cuneiform inscription.

"A new Peneus rolls his fountains
Against the evening star!"

Think of that and the Middle Western student mind. It is a murmur from an unimagined and unimaginable world. The hardwareman and the undertaker have triumphed. And their triumph is sustained in the courts of last resort. The Rockefeller Institute has made the most brazen attack on the humanities on record. No wonder! What is wanted is the skilled hand and the unresisting mind. A democracy of clever workers incapable of close thinking, ignorant of the experience of the race, can be dragged from one delusion to another, given the shadow for the substance, brow-beaten and enslaved. Yet it can, all the while, be gulled into a belief in its own freedom. Men must have heroes. The masters of steel and oil and their henchmen know that. But Milton and Shelley, Kant and Goethe are dangerous heroes. Edison is a safe one. . . . We used to argue that a civilized mind would make even an engineer a better engineer. But the capitalistic state does not want excellent engineers quite so much as it wants many engineers. It wants degrees and college graduates by the thousand. . . .

To keep what little hope I had, what impulse toward my work, I found it necessary to stop going to commencement. One year we had eight hundred graduates; we conferred eight hundred degrees. The long line passed in cap and gown. Seventy per cent should never have gotten here. Seventy per cent could stand no test—not the simplest—in fundamental thinking or judging or the elements of human knowledge. But the system is not a sieve; it's a cornucopia. . . . The faces . . . the faces . . . unformed, unstamped by any effort of thought. And then the band and the ribbons and the smug, fond parents and the revolting orators—cheap clergymen as a rule—who shout that this institution is sending forth into life the trained and chosen heralds of civilization. . . . Trained and chosen! Good Lord! Even with our enforced slackness, how did most of these raw young fools slide through? And since they did how, in the name of our as, I once thought, common nature, did they escape after four mortal years so uncontaminated by wisdom and understanding?

▼

It is clear that I have omitted so far what was a powerful factor in our situation—a faculty of nearly five-hundred. Could this group of men affect nothing? Could it in no sense lead the democracy toward better impulses and stricter standards? There was a time when I would have said yes. But the war came and, as we shall see—it is indeed notorious—these gentlemen went to pieces. But even before the war the trouble with the American professorate was its cowardice and its effeminacy of mind. Two men there were on that campus in Central City who in public writing and private speech stood four-square against the pulpiness and muddled utilitarianism of our educational machine. Just two—my friend, the professor of philosophy and I. Others agreed with us quite sincerely. We prodded them in vain. My friend is of British extraction and I of Jewish. We were free of that infinitely curious, characteristic American trait—the easy-going, kindly, disastrous dislike of clean-cut individual convictions. I emphasize the word individual. When the war came these lambs roared like lions. But then they roared in herds. In the old days they had no convictions. If they had them they would not express them. Because, observe, if you have a conviction and express it, you are by that very fact contradicting someone who thinks otherwise. And suppose—though he hasn't whispered on the subject —that other one is the dean of your college! You might "hurt his feelings!" Let the republic slide to the devil. But don't let us hurt anyone's feelings. My friend and I used often to feel almost truculent when we were barely self-respecting. Our colleagues were as tepid as weak tea. . . . At the faculty language and literature club no one ever exercised sharp criticism of another's paper or report. Truth? Science? It takes "aliens" to get excited over such things. And at nine-thirty they grew restive. They were expected at home. The consummate terror in which they stood of their uninteresting wives gave the last touch to the picture of their moral and intellectual futility.

There are deeper reasons for the lack of intellectual hardihood that marks our university faculties. Who and what are these American professors? They are, almost all, honorable and high-minded gentlemen. They try, in a feeble way, to live up to the best light they have, although, as Arnold said of their ancestors, they're criminally careless about inquiring whether that light is not darkness. But they are not men driven by an inner urgency. They are not the servants of an idea or of a passion of the soul. Most of them could easily have been something else. They went into teaching either because they had a pleasant taste for learning and no particular taste for anything else; or because they were timid and of a retiring nature and didn't like the rough and tumble of the business world. Or, because—in an appalling number of cases —they simply drifted into the academic life. Thus there is among them little intensity or power, little courage or independence, much pinch-beck dignity and lust for administrative twaddle.

The argument used to be current on that campus, as it is on every campus, that strong men do not enter the academic profession because there are no prizes in it. We were, it is true, wretchedly poor. That poverty has increased year by year. Nor were we rewarded by any great dignity of social standing or approval. Yet the argument was and remains but a shallow one. The youth whose whole being is one consuming and unanswerable passion for literature or science or philosophy, who shrinks at the very thought of business or money-getting, cannot be deterred from the academic life by its slender rewards. For he seeks and chooses that life in order to live at all. He must choose it at whatever salary. No; the "strong man in business" argument is a fallacy. That strong man could never have been the academic strong man. His capability of being what he is is proof enough. He did not, by an unescapable compulsion, love best the eternal things of the mind. If he did, he couldn't be spending his time in anything so trivial as making money by multiplying or exchanging things. . . . The best men in the university are those who couldn't possibly have been anything else. They are the ones whom a wise polity would not condemn to humiliating penury. They are the brains and the souls and the hope of the land. The mere teachers, who might as easily have been bank-officials or commission-merchants, are not to be pitied. Let them be other things for a few academic generations. Then perhaps the chosen servants of the eternal life will come into their own. . . . But try to urge that on a given campus. Do you mean So and So should go? Exactly! But he is such a good husband! Which means that the poor man is not only an ass but a feebly uxorious ass. . . .

It goes without saying that the majority of those who drift into the academic life are dreary specialists with, angular, strawy minds. They often teach their subjects competently in the narrow, technical sense, but without richness or savor or human and philosophical implications. Yet that is what the American student supremely needs. He needs the electric touch of personality; he gets uncoordinated information. But many of my colleagues really had a kind of pharisaism in this matter. Their attitude was: this is my specialty; I am master of it; I don't pretend to more and distrust those who do. In the early years—I grew wary later—a colleague once asked me: "What's your special line?" He knew, of course, that I was teaching German. He meant: do I specialize in the sixteenth century or the eighteenth, the Middle High German lyric or the Renaissance drama. I wasn't thinking of his psychology and answered: "Oh, in some moods I'm sorry I'm not teaching English, but I find German literature more and more sustaining as time goes on. Of course, there are advantages in—" The good man's look of cool and incredulous amazement cut my innocent outpourings short.

VI

The actual business of teaching was often dreary enough. Largely because there was no proper division of work. I taught a section of beginners and conducted a seminar for candidates for the doctorate. I taught intermediate classes. In a word, I was high school teacher, college teacher, university professor on the same day. I had constantly to practice and apply to my subject three utterly different methods. The wear and tear of that was great. It made against concentration and harmony and hence effectiveness. There was also a terrible amount of sheer, heart-breaking waste. The elective system permits a student to take just enough of a subject to illumine his special and general ignorance. But I dare say that a qualitative differentiation of work for the professors or compulsion upon the student to master something would both have been considered undemocratic and are so considered now. When I used to present such considerations my friends often thought me a pessimist, one who sees life with a jaundiced eye. They had an eighteenth centuryish kind of cheer. This is the best of all possible worlds. In our easy-going, democratic way we shall muddle through. Through? Yes. But in what direction? To what goal? Well, here we are in 1921. The best civilization on the old Continent is dying. We are fat and also the reactionaries, the Black Hundreds, of the world. My friends in Central City are, I swear, capable of not knowing or not permitting themselves to know either, but of still trying to muddle through with optimistic phrases. . . .

Yet my very pessimism sustained me, urged me on to new efforts, to the daily service of the cause. However tired I was, however discouraged, once in the class-room I felt an energy that never quite failed me. There might have been on that day one student—if but one——who heard me in the deeper sense and accepted, however imperfectly, the spirit of my teaching —one who at least in the years to come would realize through memory that once in his youth he had heard a summons from the common and the mean, a protest against the obliteration of all freer and finer values, a call to become a member of that small company of elect spirits who have been, in every age, the guardians of the torch of the true humanities. For it is by its production of such a company of spirits that a civilization stands or falls. Number and size are a monstrous delusion, machinery is a snare, wealth is trash. . . . A society which, as a whole, venerates Edison more than Emerson is in danger of becoming a society of damned souls in the only sense in which damnation has a meaning. What a platitude. Only, unfortunately, it isn't a platitude in America—it's heretical nonsense. In America, observe! Not among those Swedish and German and Levantine and Irish critics and writers in New York whose influence upon the civilization of their native land is beginning to trouble the patriots. . . .

In my moments of half-humorous despair I used to tell myself that my fine phrases did, at least, square with the brutal fact. There never was more than one such student to be found. Not in a class, but in a year. So and so many young women, of course, went through the gesture of understanding. But the gestures were quite like those they made at receptions—elegant conventions by which to hide the true state of their minds. Or else their reactions were sentimental. After an energetic lecture on the ethical problem in Faust, an immense, buxom, blank-faced young woman came languishing to my desk: "Oh, Professor, you give me such a beautiful feeling!" Such moments were discouraging. They took the wind out of one's sails. I used to cherish the ambition to teach at an institution for men only. . . .

Yet I shall not end this chapter upon so negative a note. As I said at the beginning: My students were very loyal to me. Whether they understood me or not—usually they didn't—whether I was teaching them language or literature, they felt that I was bent upon some business in which their souls were somehow really concerned. That much nearly all of them saw; for that perception they were nearly all a little grateful. So that, in addition to conveying a certain amount of knowledge, I at least did this during my seven years as a college teacher: I caused a number of young

THE BUSINESS OF EDUCATION

Americans of the Middle West to regard with liking and respect one who was frankly merciless to the popular fallacies and the mass delusions amid which they had to live.

I earned my small salary upon austerer terms than most of my colleagues. I gave myself, not only my knowledge of German. Nor was I idle during my brief leisure, full as that leisure often was of an intense anguish of body and mind. I wrote several books that brought me little money but carried the name of my university where it had not been heard before and also visibly caused juster and truer views of the subjects with which they dealt to prevail. I was, in brief, a citizen passionately and fruitfully concerned for the welfare of a society which had always received him grudgingly and half-heartedly, but which he had nevertheless come to regard as his own. And because I would not join in a cosmic orgy of stupidity and slander, of foul myth and blood-soaked ritual I was finally held to be in that place of my activity a meaner citizen than any owner of leathern lungs and brazen lips. . . .

A friend told me the other day that my name is a household word among the very cultured of Central City. They regard me and my work as, in an intimate and delightful sense, their own. . . . I didn't contradict the tepid little lady. Those people are capable of saying and feeling just that. The war is over. My reputation is growing. Why shouldn't they get a little pleasure and self-importance out of it? They have forgotten the year of grace 1917 when no hand but one was stretched out to help me, because I would not be a hypocrite and could not be a fool.

They're Anglo-Americans—these good people. They are quite sincere. They do not know the difference between truth and falsehood. If ever I visit Central City they are capable of giving a banquet—with grape-juice—in my honor. . . .

CHAPTER VIII.

THE COLOR OF LIFE

I

In the seventh month of the first year of our stay in Central City there came a special delivery letter from my father. He wrote that I must come home for a few days at once, because my mother had to undergo an operation which could not be delayed. . . . I want to describe these events without reticence. Literature has a way of veiling pain—or talking about it. We should look at pain as it is. If we are less furtive about it, perhaps we shall spend more of our strength trying to mend life, less trying to break each others' lives. . . .

Mary tried to calm me. We had been in Queenshaven that summer and my mother had seemed, as she always did, in radiant health, preserving even then a faint touch of the coloring and the freshness of youth. But in my mind some dark, actually audible gong seemed to ring out. Then the body responded. A sweetish, gnawing sickness in the pit of the stomach; a bitter dryness in the throat and mouth. For several years that condition never left me. It returns often, to this day, at the most trifling anxiety.

On the long journey South, caged in a sleeper, deprived by a brutal tyranny of the tonic and relief of wine, I shook in an uninterrupted cold fever. I had no hope . . . Queenshaven looked like a toy city in an eerie dream, my father's white face contorted into a smile of welcome looked like a goblin's. "Mother is up, perfectly strong." He tried to put a reassuring note into this statement. But the trouble was—well? Yes, cancer. Far gone. In a most vital spot. I nearly doubled up with the sweetish gnawing in my entrails. I tried to speak, but my mouth seemed to be filled with lime. My father, patient and brave as always, reminded me: "Mother is up, you understand. We must. . . ." A fierce light flared up in my brain. "Of course we must!" She wasn't going to the hospital till the next day. She wanted first to spend twenty-four hours with me. . . .

She stood at the head of the stairs as always when I came home with the soft lamplight on her beautiful, white hair. But she was erect and her skin was smooth as a girl's. Only a touch of paleness. . . . I put my arms about her and dared not weep. No, somewhere within me I, too, found the strength to play my part. We smiled and chatted and even ate. But all the while I had a queer sensation. I heard my voice and the words I spoke as though they came from another speaker in the farthest corner of the room. Whenever she left us alone, my father and I fell silent and our contorted faces relaxed and we rested as men catch their breath in the intervals of torture. . . . On the evening of that day—a calm, bland day—we drove her to the infirmary. She was rather stunned and rather frightened. She had hardly ever known illness. But the room assigned seemed pleasant to her, the special nurse was a sturdy, sensible Scotch girl and the Mother Superior who knew us and had some insight into our situation was quite perfect in her serious, hopeful sweetness. . . .

The operation, next morning, lasted for over an hour. My father and I walked up and down in front of the building. We lit one cigarette from another and paced and paced. We didn't say anything. Now and then we caught each others' eyes and looked away quickly. We couldn't bear what we saw. At last the Mother Superior stood in the doorway. From her smile we knew that the operation had been successful. I couldn't smile back and she looked at me questioningly. But I was beyond self-deception and easy consolation and all the softer feelings by which people try to bear the unbearable. I knew that my mother, being strong, would probably stand the operation, however radical, well; I knew that the surgeons were excellent. I also knew, however, that there wasn't a chance of the lymphatic system not being badly involved and that before many months my mother would die—would die by slow, intolerable poisoning, with all her hopes frustrated—would die before I had had a chance to bring any brightness to her saddened heart. My old race against fate and death was lost.

I was able to stay for ten days. All day I sat beside her. She was feeling quite well. We had long talks, her hand in mine. She had never taken the morbid interest in disease that is so common, and was full of hope for the future. So even these talks that made her happy were a long torment to me. The fatal truth kept beating in my head like a pulse. Then I had to go. . . .

The next six months! Words are used up like dull, cracked, edgeless knives. They cannot cleave to those depths of pain in which, in the very centre of his being, without any reservation, a man desires his death. During the first four months there was the added sting, the withering irony, of good reports and cheerful letters to write. It seemed—things being as they were—almost more merciful when she began to sicken—when she came to us to Central City, glad to be there, still not without hope, though very ill and broken. And it seemed more merciful, too, that when she could no longer raise herself up and her anguish became so acute as to require powerful narcotics—that then she sank more swiftly into exhaustion than our physicians had predicted and, on the noon of a brilliant October day, died in Mary's arms. In the coffin she looked young again and her face wore an expression of serenity and severe sweetness which I had not seen on it for many years. . . .

During many weeks, as a matter of instinctive self-preservation, I sought refuge in certain idealistic assumptions and speculations. I re-read The Critique of the Practical Reason and even Browning. But it was merely the kind of gesture by which a man tries to ward off blows he is too weak to endure. The tentative and half-prayerful aspiration toward some extra-mundane source of power and good which had remained with me from my Christian youth died out entirely. I saw the world in a harder and a drier mood. I lost my last shred of respect for all religious and ethical formulations—for all types of supernaturalism and absoluteness in thinking—for everything except such forms of beauty or freedom or justice as might

mitigate our stark wretchedness on earth. It seemed
to me then, as it seems to me now, unspeakably monstrous that, in a world where people are poisoned by
cancer, they should persecute each other by social distinctions, ill-apportioned wealth, ethical bickering or
rob each other of a moment's peace in the brief, pitiful
sunlight in the name of any absolutist formulary, legal
or moral or religious. That sounds crude. But I am
not writing a philosophical treatise. And I am sure
that a description of the source in concrete experience
from which most philosophic and all poetic visions of
the sum of reality spring, would sound just as crude.
In a word, I abandoned all faith in any form of personal and transcendental idealism and gradually
adopted the hope for economic security and personal
freedom embodied in the revolutionary movement of
our period. No, I am not, like a good many liberals,
shirking the name of Socialism. But I would break
with Socialism as swiftly as with any other system, if
it were not to confine the power of society over the individual strictly to the sphere of economics, hygiene
and the necessity—not the character!—of education;
if it were not to leave the personal and moral life of
the individual absolutely free. I mean absolutely. I
do not mean that hoary iniquity, that vile excuse for
conscription and sex-slavery known as "liberty, oh,
yes—but no licence." I mean that every man shall
practice his own liberty, even though it seems licence
to another. I want a world—to return to that burning
symbol in my personal life—in which the beautiful,
sensitive, gifted spirit of my mother would not have
been warped and crippled by mean anxieties and social
exclusions and absurd ethical inhibitions, but one in

which she could have lived the years that the dark powers behind the veil permitted her in freedom and richness and the expansion of all her tastes and sensibilities. And I think this outlook on life well-established. It is not founded on speculation or tradition, but on the granite basis of a tragic fact.

II

So I became, naturally, more concerned with society and more watchful of it. Before this I had been almost wholly engrossed in art and thought and learning. I now turned my attention upon this city and state in which I lived and on the way in which my fellow-citizens were managing their affairs and mine.

A mayor was to be elected. The city had then over two hundred thousand inhabitants. Its government entailed some very difficult engineering problems. Also, it was and is dispiriting in its ugliness. There was its educational machine. There were other intricate matters. Now for this difficult office of mayor we had six candidates: a business man, a printer, a bank official, the chief of police, two lawyers. Let me omit the two lawyers. I knew little about them except the fact of their obscurity before election time and that neither had a chance of being elected. Of the other four, one of whom was elected, I can make certain very definite assertions: they knew nothing of municipal engineering, nothing of education, nothing of the elements of even the conventional doctrines of political science, nothing of the experiments tried in the city-government of other countries. In a word, they had no equipment for the office to which they aspired. Nor was it likely that these elderly, semi-illiterate men would equip themselves either during the brawling campaign months or during their two years in office. The stock reply of the conventional American is: Lincoln had no education either. True. But mankind doesn't produce a certain type of moral genius by the thousand. It can produce well-trained and intelligent officials. You cannot administer a commonwealth by waiting for miracles. Those four candidates, at all events, hadn't any claims to being democratic saviors of society. On the contrary. They were men of the coarsest fibre—men with spiritually dead faces, with something gross and callous, impudent and yet furtive about their personalities and bearing. They exhibited a curious, I had almost said, family resemblance in this respect. And it was ghastly to see how these men, in the poster photographs during the campaign, had tried to look the part expected of them— benevolent and honest, "smart" and burly. The pictures seemed to want to say to the voter: "Don't think I pretend to know more than you. I worked hard as a boy and supported my pore ol' mother. I never had no time for book- learnin'. But I've got a certain amount of plain common sense, Mr. Voter, and business experience and these I want to put at your disposal. And I'm a jolly good fellow."

In their speeches and proclamations these four candidates made the same assertions. Each was going to give the city an honest administration—no graft— (as if that were a positive virtue, as if it weren't shameful that the voter should have to choose on that plane)—each was going to give us a clean city—(by which he meant making life a bit more difficult for a

few hundred prostitutes)—each was going to give us
an efficient and economical administration. Very well.
Only every one knew that none of the men had the
equipment or the purity of will to do either. As a matter of fact the candidates wanted office either because
they thought it would help them in a business way or
through meanly personal ambition or because they had
been accustomed to make their bread and butter out of
a political job. Seeing their character, it was not difficult to imagine what concessions and promises each
made quite inevitably to the business men and finan-
ciers who backed him and provided the machinery and
funds for his campaign.

All this sounds commonplace enough. And indeed
it is. But I came upon it with a certain freshness, a
certain innocence, an ability to be shocked by the
brazen and meaningless clatter of it. The world has
moved since then. But the character of political government in the affairs of cities and of states has not
changed. Its purpose is to deceive the common folk
and to fortify and extend the power of the privileged
classes. And since power ultimately means economic
power, since its one source is possession—possession
of land, tools, means of transportation—it follows that,
consciously or unconsciously, the whole function and
intent of political government is to keep possession and
hence power in the hands of those that now hold it.
And since this oligarchy controls the press and thus
controls both the news and opinion based on news, it is
clear that its self-perpetuation will not be broken—has
not been broken in any country—without some final
catastrophe.

THE COLOR OF LIFE

II

Have we, I asked in those years, no directer expression of the popular will. Yes. In matters that are non-political, therefore non-economic and so moderately indifferent to the possessing classes—in education (though even here, as I have shown, it is to the profit of the oligarchs to confirm popular folly) and in the government of the personal life of men. Every two years in those days the people of the state voted on a prohibition amendment to the constitution; every two years it was defeated by a smaller minority. To-day we have national prohibition. New York liberals wonder how it could have happened. They should have watched the paralysis of will and impulse creeping over a Middle Western state, a state full of what has recently become known as the "home-town."

Each time the question came up I found my Anglo-American friends succumbing a little more and a little less willing to protest against the raucous propaganda. It became in the end almost "bad form." In the first place, twenty-one states were already dry—even Michigan. So the terrible fatalism of democracy, inherent in its worship of majority opinion and its fundamental rejection of qualitative distinctions was making itself felt more and more. If a disease spreads, expose yourself to it. Why should you want something better than others? I found my acquaintances almost so sodden in their folly. Furthermore—it was a question of morals and they had an unconquerable hesitation toward taking a negative attitude on a question of morals. Even those who were not at all fanatical and themselves drank were willing to let things take their evil course: "It does nobody any good; it does some people harm; I mustn't be selfish. ..." They looked at me with estranged eyes when I said: "I'd be willing to take an oath never to touch fermented liquor again if only I could save our people from the infamy of prohibition."

But most of my friends were, in some strange way, hypnotized by the fevered fanatics of the Anti-Saloon League and the Evangelical Churches. No one seemed to understand the character of these poor creatures. They can no longer burn witches or whip Quakers. They have somehow lost their grip on the devil of old. So they have made the substance known as ethyl alcohol into an overshadowing myth—the evil thing in the world that must be fought and trodden under foot and exorcised by Christian men. Since they cannot quite in this age say that I am an unbelieving dog, they say—with sternly pitying and averted faces—that I shall die a drunkard. It is, of course, because in their savage and yet festering souls they have never caught a glimpse of the meaning of humane culture— choice, self-direction, a beautiful use of all things. These poor slaves of drink must either howl against it or reel in barrooms. One knows the type: thin-lipped, embittered by the poisons that unnatural repression breeds, with a curious flatness about the temples, with often, among the older men, a wiry, belligerent beard. You have seen them with their shallow-bosomed, ill-favored wives—stern advocates of virtue—walking on Sunday self-consciously to church. The wine they have never tasted, the white beauty they have never seen, the freedom of art they have never known—all their

unconscious hungers have turned to gall and worm-
wood in their crippled souls.

Yet to these maimed creatures—a bodily cripple
is a more wholesome sight—my friends in Central
City yielded more and more. They yielded to them
in all matters. A film was shown down town that Mary
and I wanted to see. It was useless. Before we could
go, the secretary of the Lord's Day Association had
caused it to be mutilated in the interest of our moral
being. . . . I wanted to buy another copy of Dreiser's
The Genius. It had been forbidden by the Society for
the Prevention of Vice. I am not able, as some of my
liberal New York friends are, to take a humourous
view of this situation. To take that view of it is to be
in danger of supineness. Consider the matter clearly:
We are helpless against any irresponsible person who
shouts: Morality, Purity, the Home. Yet precisely
these difficult and rigid concepts must be broken before
a ray of civilization can light our gloom. For en-
tangled in them, tightly woven into them, is an amount
of concrete human tyranny, concrete human suffering
—days of despair and nights of agony—that is probably unexampled in history. The emotional acceptance
of these concepts has diminished even where a helplessness of the mind curbs the formation of a conscious
protest. The result is dumb misery and perversion
and the sickening and putrefaction of the impulses of
will and sex. When psychical explosions come, they
necessarily take the form of war, hate, persecution,
lynching. Degraded by the oppression of Morality
and Purity and the Home—in their current mean-
ings—men summon the evil passions bred by their
degradation to defend its instruments. . . .

UP STREAM

IV

In our early years in Central City Mary and I used to go out into society a good deal. Later we acquired a reputation for refusing invitations. I could endure no more. For what was the use of going to places if other people only sent their clothes and manners and left their real selves at home. It was, at best, a pantomime, a ceremony, a decorative device. I cannot say that most of our acquaintances in Central City were successful decorations. Stereotyped phrases fluttered in the air; ice-cream was served. The phrases sickened me; so did the ice-cream.

What wore on me most was the appalling mental vacuity. People said they were having a pleasant time. Some lied. Others had sunk so low that their remark was true. Since I, as a teacher and writer, was supposed to have an official connection with the arts, the women talked art at me—poetry and the drama. Cold chills used to run down my spine. "Art, my good ladies, is not what you suppose: it's not a game—like bridge; it's not a ceremony—like a reception. It is the record and clarification of deepest human experience. It raises into permanence and beauty for our contemplation the experience of man upon his way. Think of the day you saw your mother die, of the hours you lay in bitter labor with your first-born, of the moment when you came, a virgin, to a man's embrace. These are sources of art. Or have you ever been hungry or an outcast or fought single-handed in a good cause?" If I had ever said that! "Don't you think, doctor, that X. is a *wonderful* writer?" "Of course, you ought to know, but *I* think. . .

[188]

think. . . ." So they twittered and chirped—elderly
women, too, mothers who ought to have come into some
earnestness with the years. They had. Only the life
of art and of the intellect is not a serious matter to
them and their kind. Money is a serious matter. Social position is another. Health is a third. Then why,
in God's name, didn't they talk money and social position and disease? Why were they not a little truthful?
I don't care about money and social position and I
hate to talk about disease except when I must and then
to a doctor. Yet everything human is interesting, so
it be forthright and comes from a deep source. . . .
But that's bad form. "Oh, I thought your lecture last
week *so* stimulating." She probably lied and I felt
like asking her what my lecture was about. Instead I
had to grin over my abominable ice-cream and say with
the proper intonation: "So nice of you to have come
to it." No, I abandoned that sort of thing and went,
instead, to a public-house with a friend. It was so
much more decent. Of course, I was popularly
credited with a tinge of vulgarity. But the people
forgave me. Even those who didn't never let Mary
feel it. Until the war came they were kindly enough.
. . . The men, at these affairs, were largely background.
They followed the lead of the women. There was a
touch of mild, middle-aged archness. Flirting would
be too gross a word. There was no liberty of mind or
emotion or personality or speech.

The men alone present a different aspect. I was,
for instance, invited to a private and exclusive little
club of business-men and bankers and lawyers and
physicians. The club met at a rich man's house. The
place was furnished with luxury and in tolerably good

taste. There was beer and tobacco and an atmosphere of virile ease. It looked hopeful. Nearly all the men had a local reputation for culture and were graduates of Eastern colleges. Yet, as the evening wore on, I grew more and more silent and when it was over I was glad to get out into the cool, dark street alone. For these men talked exclusively of things—the price of real estate, of stocks and bonds and sugar. They told stories of shady business deals and of political corruption. Not, be it observed, in a spirit of criticism, but with acquiescent good humor. The monstrous implication of all their talk—I include both the distinguished occulist and the learned judge—was this: here we have the best of all polities in the best of all possible worlds; for in this polity and in this world we make our money and have these houses and automobiles and fifty-cent cigars. Anyone, therefore, who wants to change this order is a knave or a fool and we would go to any length to crush him. Well-fed, well-groomed, they sat in their impenetrable stolidity, taking liberties with everything except their minds. The gentleness which they had at receptions was quite gone. There was something agate-like about them. I understood at last how it is possible for men to hire thugs and incite striking workers to violence and then shoot them down. In mellower intervals they talked golf and base-ball. . . . They treated me with finished courtesy. But their courtesy didn't hide their essential attitude: I was to them (by virtue of the interests I stood for) a little higher than a fiddler, many degrees lower, except socially, than "Babe" Ruth. They didn't mind an occasional condescension to art and learnings. But these things are really, they seemed to say,

luxuries for women. Nor did their own assertion of
personal freedom—the excellent beer they drank—en-
courage one. For they drank only at private houses
and private clubs. They drank with an evil secretive-
ness and a poisonous aloofness. Quite conceivably
they voted "dry." Their clubs are still supplied—
you may be sure. The decent and the democratic places
to drink are home—with open windows—and the public-house. But a genuine as opposed to a pseudo-demo-
cratic bearing might have injured their financial
standing, their professional dignity. In public they
all talk liberty. In reality they were stealthier than
feudal lords. Later, no doubt, they became the sup-
porters of Navy Clubs and Defense Leagues and of
the modern Inquisition under Mitchel Palmer. . . .

v

Is there no rebellion against the dark unveracity
that degrades and muffles all the instincts of man?
Faint flutterings—pathetic in the sense of their own
feebleness and shame. Has any other people ever
expressed its Dionysiac mood so spiritlessly as in jazz,
the new dances, the common cabaret? And yet . . .
listen well to this raucous, syncopated music—not
music so much as sheer, rude rhythm—like the stamping feet and clapping hands of rude, old orgiastic folk-
dances. Now and then, in the tunes, you come upon a
vain and melancholy cry—a cry of torment, a cry of
liberation. Read the words of the popular songs—
sung in a million parlors every evening by shop-girls,
typists, laundresses, even college-girls to their

[191]

"beaux." They are illiterate and vulgar and indescribably mean. But what imperious instinct cursed and beaten into hiding will not show the ugly marks of the slave? The choruses of these songs are ugly because they dare not be beautiful, stealthy because they dare not be frank. But in dance and song and ragtime there is a craving for rhythm—the rhythm of the world that is sex and poetry and freedom. It is an ugly, hoarse, tortured rhythm—like the dancing of a crippled child. . . . The rhythm beats on and on. . . .

My friend the lawyer told me this story from the records of the Central City courts. A fellow killed a man and was sent to prison. His young wife supported herself and her child and her mother and faithfully waited for her husband. He came out of prison and beat her and ran away and was heard of no more. So the young woman and her mother took a lodger. He fell in love with the woman and they lived together. He supported her and her mother and her child. But when his own child was born the court arrested the couple, sentenced them to the workhouse for adultery and placed the children in public institutions. The records do not tell us what became of the old mother, nor in what state of mind the man and woman came from the workhouse. Do you wonder that to the people love has come to seem a shameful thing? . . . Men sit at cheap burlesque shows with a leer. Why not? Judges and clergymen and businessmen tell them that their appetites—the source of all they have in life of poetry and romance and the freedom of choice and adventure —are bestial; that they are not—the last ingenuity of foulness—to be humanized, but to be whipped out of sight like mangy curs. Then they expect them to be clean and handsome. . . . The man and the woman of my story came out, I suppose, with a purer love, a cleaner sex-life, a higher self-respect. . . . We shall not have lovelier private morals until we have destroyed public morality—the fang and claw of Puritan capitalism. . .

There are nobler protests and more conscious ones than dances and cabarets. There is the rebellion of the intellect and of a few free personalities. Little groups of men and women detach themselves from the monotonous mass here and there. People jeer at Greenwich Village—the shabby Latin Quarter of New York. Even liberals are contemptuous. But do you expect anything unstained and clear to-day? Even this is something. The other day, after a long interval, I wrote some verses. And they sum up something of this whole matter. I called the verses The Greenwich Villagers and represented these people as speaking of themselves:

We're shabby and not always clean. We know. . . .
You come from Harlem and from Washington Heights
And look at us as though we were a show,
And crowd through foolish little inns for sights,
And, being liberals, are sorry for
Our fluttering aims and large futility. . . .
And when the lamps go out we seem to be
Hovering shadows in a dim corridor
That leads to places where a man forgets
Amid the blue fume of the cigarettes
Man's proper business for which earth was made:
Marriage and war and trade.

But just because we do forget, because
In our small, callow, ineffectual way
We drift beyond success and all its laws
And warm our hearts with brief loves as the day
Dips red in the North River—therefore we
Are as a flicker of hope above the gray
Walls of your goodness and brutality.

We are the children of the land who fled
In Autumn when the winds of longing blew
Even from Pittsburgh and from Kalamazoo
From jobs in which our brothers served and rose,
From colleges with Doric porticoes
Where living things are fettered to things dead—
And we are nothing but the unresigned
Who in great darkness feebly speak the name
Of that rebellion which will save mankind
And from our poor, lost ashes leap to flame.

And so you may despise us more or less,
And hug your righteousness and your success,
And never dream that we poor lads in blue,
We girls with draggled skirts and close-bobbed hair
May be the saving of the souls of you,
Even as we tramp on Greenwich Avenue
Or loiter in the dusk on Washington Square.

But these things were far from Central City. Faint
rumors came. What, in those years, I definitely knew
and saw was the Federal Post Office stamping out as
either "seditious" or "obscene" anything it pleased.
From 1915 on the silence deepened—an ugly ominous
silence. Such, I dare say, was the silence in the Inquisition chambers. Also, men began to break off
speech in the middle of a sentence and turn a little red
or pale. And they began to watch each other and fur-
tively to listen to each other for seditious remarks and

plan and scheme how they could make business or professional profit out of their neighbor's indiscretion. And anonymous letters and telephone calls kept busy the offices of the District Attorney, who, although we were to be "kept out of the war," was very accessible to information that might come in handy later. . . .

VI

Yet then and even now the man on the streets thinks that we have liberty. He has no true conception of its nature, and his spirit is corrupted by the brutal romanticism of success. For he is right in thinking that, within ever narrowing limits, he has one kind of liberty—the liberty of economic competition. He may, if he is clever and unscrupulous enough, steal the resources that belong to all men and so enslave a number of his fellows and become a plutocrat himself. He reads about Morgan and Rockefeller and shakes his head with a leer: "Smart men." And perhaps he has a day-dream of himself—now working at thirty-five a week and rent going up and the children without shoes—and well, who knows? He may himself "put through a little deal" some day and live "on easy street!" He wouldn't vote the Socialist ticket for hell! Why, look at So and So! Started at eight a week. Now he's president of the Great Gorge Road. Worth five millions if he's worth a cent. The man pushes back his greasy derby and spits with a speculative air. "Smart people in this here world, I tell you." His wife reads her Sunday paper and glows over accounts of the social doings of the local plutocrats. She drops her paper and dreams the same day-dream from another angle. And the cheap magazines that float their way and the picture-shows they see all glorify wealth and "getting on" and yet carefully refrain from arousing any social consciousness. For generally the old millionaire repents and sinks into a pool of domestic emotions and gives his daughter in marriage to the poor young man. And our citizen's wife nudges her husband and points to the young man on the screen who is just about to marry the millionaire's daughter and says: "Ain't he the perfect image of our Johnny?"

Our man has the liberty of economic competition. Of the slimness of his chance to avail himself of that liberty he does not think. He can dream his favorite dream. Also he has a vote. He can choose between two candidates both offered him by essentially the same masters. Also he can worship at either the Baptist Church or the Methodist or the Campbellite. But once let him think and arise from the dull mass and cease worshipping the idols of the tribe and the market-place! If he speaks he will be gagged; if he acts he will be jailed. Yet it is only for that arisen and awakened man that liberty has its true meaning. When the personal consciousness emerges from the merely tribal consciousness—there is the birth of liberty. Hence in a deeper sense the common phrase is true: liberty means progress—the liberty of individuals to rebel against the mass-life, to repudiate mass-thinking, to shatter the folk-ways, to be the instruments of change. A society in which majority opinion and public law have not risen to the tolerance of such free personalities is a society without liberty and without hope from within. It may build machinery and heap up wealth. It is as stagnant as a rotting pool.

One hears people talk fatuously about "evolution" not revolution. They are usually of the economic master class. What they mean is the preservation of the *status quo*. They hope that they will always be able to gather enough votes and control enough candidates and own enough land and tools and ships and trains to perpetuate the present order exactly as it is. Thus they defeat the hope of orderly change and create the revolutionary spirit. For they stigmatize each step in the developmental process as revolutionary. And since all ultimate change is reached by successive changes, since, in a word, the evolutionary process consists of a series of revolutions, they rob themselves, by their own unveracity and muddleheadedness, of the easements in the process of change which might well be theirs. Hence, though they may delay their fall, they refuse foolishly to mitigate its horrors. It is, an old story. Men do not learn by experience, as I have said. Nor is it easy for them to believe that to be true which contradicts their interests and their hopes. We all share that weakness—capitalist and proletarian, business-man and intellectual. But there are minds which, having seen their hopes go down to incredible disaster once, walk thereafter more warily and humbly in the world and see the drift of things which will not change for their liking and read coldly, without regard to their hearts and desires, the signs that flame in the cosmic skies.

CHAPTER IX

Myth and Blood

I

In August the grass on the campus looked singed, the trees and bushes stale. In the halls the graduate students, registered for summer school, raised a clatter that was somehow drained of energy. They went through all the motions of intense life, but the inner principle was lacking. White skirts, filmy bodices, filmier stockings. Firm bodies that throbbed. But the outer mind, carefully trained in the mimicry of self-preservation, pursued points of pedagogical technique with a bitter eagerness. A few were old and quiet. There was also one small, consumptive-looking Chinaman with a cold, remorseless appetite for knowledge. He seemed to gnaw at my brain. The dusty class-rooms pulsed with the hot air and the bodies of the young women. "When one is young"—I was discussing Schnitzler in my seminar that summer of 1914—"life is full of windows and beyond every window the world begins." That saying seemed a ferocious irony in Central City. We moved in a cruel hush behind black bars. Our windows were all prison windows.

There were no signs in the heavens. There never are. Only I remember one dry, blazing noon looking intently at the stripped and wilted lilac bushes and saying to myself: "Little Servia." It must have been July. In August it would have been: "Little Belgium." Those phrases are cheap and ugly and tattered to-day. They are like the styles of a decade ago. No one is saying: "Little Hayti." They are out of fashion but lacking in the dignity of age; they are ugly without quaintness, like shoulder-of-mutton sleeves. Some day they will flame once more for that small community of spirits which remembers and records the vicissitudes of mankind. Then it will be written down how huge populations devoid of gallantry or mercy, aching themselves through their emissaries to dabble in the blood of any at their feet—in Amritsar or Balbriggan, Hayti or North Africa, Jewish villages in Poland or black belt towns in Georgia—took up the cry of "Hun" and poisoned the minds of young people and little children on three continents not against the fierce competitions that end in hate and blood, but against the soul of the German people. It will be written down in the history books. But to the man and woman on the street historic truth is pragmatic. Truth is what prevails. That is one reason why I think this Christian-capitalistic civilization will be overturned. At its core festers a cancerous lie. It feeds on spiritual tissue. The superstructure will decay. . . .

I shall not fight the war over. ⟨A mind that does not see it to-day as universal guilt or else universal blundering and fatality and does not mourn over every portion of mankind with an intensity measured purely by that portion's acuteness of suffering, is beyond the reach of reason and humanity.⟩ I find a good many people admitting that now, but often with a shadow of mental reservation. Aren't we, their eyes seem to plead, a little, oh, just a little better than the Germans —just we and the British? That plea, that look, is fatal. Only by giving up self-righteousness to the last shred, only by an utter and universal brotherhood in self-abasement can anything be saved from the wreckage. For those with that look in their eyes and also to steady and keep true the drift of this story which is not only a story but a symbol I recall and record:

The German militarists commanded the fighting to be done with merciless severity.

British troops before going into action were habitually given the following instructions: "The second bayonet man kills the wounded. You cannot afford to be encumbered by wounded enemies lying about your feet. Don't be squeamish. The army provides you with a good pair of boots; you know how to use them." (Stephen Graham: A Private of the Guards.)

From 1917 on the German High Command used wildly desperate and brutal measures to win the war.

From the autumn of 1917 on, the hunger blockade, which the government of the United States called "illegal and indefensible" in 1914, produced rachitis, a change and softening of the bony structure among the civilian population of Germany. The chief sufferers were children under five, adolescents between fourteen and eighteen and women over forty. The little children became crippled and could not walk; the girls and boys crumpled up in the streets; the women died.

The Germans had lost the ancient tradition of a chivalrous respect for one's foes.

MYTH AND BLOOD

It was during their final retreat in 1919. " 'I must admit that the boche is a tenacious brute.' said a young French lieutenant just back from the firing line. 'This Grand Division has been smashed to pieces, yet the remnant fights just as hard. Cornered rats, I suppose. Anyway, it shows that their discipline is still strong, that men will sell their lives thus without hope!' " (The New York Times, July 31, 1919.)

The armies of the allies went forth to defeat a menacing militarism. They believed what they were told.

The Germans "were men fighting blindly to guard an ideal, the Heimat, some patch of mother earth. . . . This everything that meant home to them they were told was in danger, and this they went out to save." (Evelyn, Princess Blücher: An English Wife in Berlin.)

Lissauer wrote a Song of Hate, Regnier wrote Serment, our population went to a propaganda film: The Beast of Berlin.

Thackeray recalls the wars against Napoleon in his lecture on George III. "We prided ourselves on our prejudices; we blustered and bragged with absurd vainglory; we dealt to our enemy a monstrous injustice of contempt and scorn; we fought them with all weapons, mean as well as heroic. There was no lie we would not believe, no charge of crime which our furious prejudice would not credit. I thought at one time of making a collection of the lies which the French had written against us and we had published against them during the war: it would be a strange memorial of popular falsehood."

A universal brotherhood of self-abasement!

In Central City invisible pulses began to beat all about me in the air. I wrote: All the few hard-won virtues of the free personality are going down to disaster. The individual was merciful; the tribe is callous. The individual was reasonable; the tribe is in the grip of dark, irrational instincts. Thus public passions, however generous their apparent origin, degenerate into wild unreason and bestiality. A public passion of religion sees miracles; a public passion of hatred sees atrocities. Both are well attested in all countries and in all ages of a religious or a war-like mood. Immemorial savage impulses which the individual dare not express are vented under the supposed righteousness of a tribal sanction and decent men become persecutors, lynchers and murderers. Such, from any civilized point of view, is the basic tragedy of war. The merging of the individual into the tribe wipes out all the difficult gains of the cultural process. It hurls us back into the red, primordial mists of hate and cruelty and self-righteousness. The imaginative vision comes to see and hear in the tense atmosphere of still peaceful cities symbolical scenes of a forgotten age—the flashing cymbals, the foaming devotees, the shrill scream of the human sacrifice in the storm-shaken grove. . . .

The great myth crystalized with a suddenness that took one's breath away. A quick, thunderous passion for a living sacrifice flared up. I am persuaded that any other object would have served equally well. Nearly all my colleagues in Central City owed the sounder part of their intellectual equipment to German sources; many had endearing memories of the German land and its people. These potent subjective realities were submerged at once. The flood, then, was one that had always been pounding in the darkness against the dykes of the mind. Historic accident or fatality made a breach. The waters swirled.

They all led—the great, decent, American middle-classes, business and professional—rigid and unnatural lives. They led and still lead unreal lives. In France, in Germany, in Italy, the same official codes and forms prevail. But there the forms are large-meshed nets; here they are cages of concrete and steel. The respectable American unless he is quite rich cannot take a moral holiday. Even when he takes it, his nature is so inhibited and corrupted by an unreal morality that his holiday becomes a debauch. He usually marries rather early and marries a woman nearly or quite his own age. Three or four children are born. When the man is forty, his wife has no freshness left. She is a little wrinkled and without emotional resilience. It is tragic for the women, more tragic than for the men. But they refuse compassion or cure by refusing to admit the reality of the tragic facts. They insist on what they call equal marriages and as they fade demand more stonily the rigidness of the home as due to their cooperation, their social worth, the sacred service of their motherhood. It is very astute of them. They deny out of existence the wildness of nature. The churches aid them. The men, who are not thinkers, are deceived into hideous repressions or ugly debauches and either become insensitive or battle with a foolish sense of sin.

It will be thought degraded to attribute the out-

burst of so-called patriotic passion that swept this
country in any degree to the sex-repressions practised
by our middle-classes. But it was not due to terror
and revengefulness as in France, nor to terror and
ambition as in Germany. Nor were there historic
hatreds or old feuds or national memories involved.
Many elements unquestionably contributed to it. But
its peculiarly unmotivated ferocity, its hectic heat had
in it something unmistakably religious, orgiastic and
hence obscurely sexual. Upon Germany, the vicarious
sacrifice, was heaped all secret horror and shame and
corruption, to her were transferred all hidden sins and
rebellions and perversities. The nation became a
lynching party. Its mood expressed itself spontane-
ously through sex-symbolism. The rape of Belgium!
In propaganda films and plays, the German villain
was always represented as seeking the defloration of
American virgins. Faith, blood, sadism—an old trin-
ity. If this is ignoble it is because human nature is so.
Or, rather, because man through a pathetic delusion in-
sists that what in him is natural is ignoble. The fact
remains. Neither proletarians nor plutocrats were as
hectic, were as sick in soul with the war fever as the
intelligent, moral, thoughtful bourgeoisie. The campus
in Central City became like an infected place. The
young students were quite cool and sane. The middle-
aged professors with homely and withered wives and
strong moral opinions shouted and flared up and
wreaked themselves on William II—and Kant and
Nietzsche and Wagner and even Eucken. When they
saw me their eyes glowed strangely or turned fiercely
cold. I would not join the lynching-party. I had a
weakness for the lynchee. . . . I was regarded as

good, loyal Southerners—guardians of Christianity, morality, democracy—regard a "nigger-lover." The parallel is exact.

III

Yet my weakness for the lynchee was wholly unpolitical in character. It included neither Prussian pastors nor Prussian soldiers nor Bavarian priests and ultramontanes, even as my sympathies cannot include England's Black and Tan constabulary or vulgar imperialists or the fierce parsons of our own Protestant churches. If, as I freely admitted, I did not wish to see the empire stricken and abased, it was because it happened to be the temporary vessel, however imperfect, however riddled with flaws, of a spirit of civilization which seemed to me then and seems to me now of a sovereign preciousness both in itself and also for all mankind. I can illustrate my meaning best from the present moment. The year is 1921. The reparations committee is sitting in Paris seeking to reconcile the extortion of an incalculable indemnity from the German people with a permanent crippling of that people's industries, shipping, power and wealth. The republic that signed the peace of Versailles is discredited at home and abroad; the lost provinces writhe under a tyranny compared to which the stupid Polish policy of the empire was merciful and enlightened; the cities and industrial districts of what was, seven years ago, the most orderly and the healthiest country in recorded history are gaunt with hunger and rotten with disease. In Berlin, the profiteers celebrate a witches' sabbath of wild and desperate debauchery. The bureaucratic classes who

lived with dignity and security under the old order are
in a state of suicidal reactionary fervor; the workers
are too hungry and enfeebled to revolt. Fallen from
a position of boundless power and respect and intellectual preeminence in the world, this nation is hum-
bled as none has been in modern times. She is in the
dust and every demagogue and fool the world over can
void his venom on her. Old poets spoke of the terrors
of the thing they called Mutability and celebrated the
tragic circumstances of the fall of even the weakest
and vilest princes. Who, among men, can withhold
from a proud and gifted people a sombre and remorse-
ful sympathy? And yet. . . . A strange thrill of life
is running through all those stricken German lands.
Matthew Arnold called that minority which reflects
and transcends the passions and lives creatively the
saving remnant. In Germany the saving remnant has
always been large and it is large to-day. Fools and
mere tribesmen crowd the cities and citadels, but each
of these places can be saved not by one righteous man
but by a thousand. It seems ironic enough to use the
word righteous; for righteous in a rigid sense and
according to standards that antedate experience is
precisely what these people are not. What they have
done is to rend inner veils and to substitute for the
moral nominalism which is the ultimate source of the
world's sickness a vision that discerns men and things
and actions in their real and unique and incomparable
nature. They have offered defiance to that gigantic
Beast which Dante saw passing mountains, breaking
through walls and weapons, polluting the whole world
—that uncleanly image of Fraud whose face is the

face of a just man, so mild is its aspect, but whose body
is the body of a foul serpent.

> La faccia sua era faccia d'uom giusto,
> tanto benigna avea di fuor la pelle;
> e d'un serpente tutto l'altro fusto.

Life is far deeper and more intricate than most
people permit themselves to know. They make it
shallow and simple by formulations: a man can love
but one woman; guilt must be punished; we must be
unselfish. Out of these formulations and others like
them they build bridges over the abyss of the soul.
But the bridges are bridges of ice which only a careful
chill can preserve. A day comes on which the deeps
begin to glow and the bridge bursts and there is chaos.
The Germans of whom I was thinking had gone on
quests into those deeps. They are going on those quests
now. They were careless of the character of the polity
in which they lived before the war; I am not sure that
they are building their new one with a very practical
wisdom. But polities crumble and one form of the
state succeeds another and so far man has invented
none that is not irrational and tyrannical at its core.
The best we can achieve is an inner freedom, moral
and intellectual liberty, the power of standing above
the state, face to face with essential things. It is not
only the poets and the thinkers of Germany who have
done that, but undistinguished and unrecorded men by
the million—teachers and traders and waiters and
workingmen. When they talk they talk about life, not
about dead formulae, about the feelings and the
thoughts that are, not about those they would have

others entertain. In 1916 a very humble German said
to me: "Life is curious. I was a socialist in the old
country and I've got no use for the government. No,
and I don't believe in conscription. So I didn't think
I'd have any trouble at all. But when people talk to
me about the war, they and I talk about different
things altogether. They talk about militarism and
Prussianism and they don't mean anything, good or
bad, that really exists. They mean something they've
made up out of their own minds. And when I tell them
facts—mixed facts—because the world isn't a simple
place, is it?—they're mad at me because I know something definite and real and they call me a damned
Hun." And another very plain man who came to me
said: "I'm in trouble with my boss, an American
gentleman, because I had a love affair with a girl in
the shop. 'But you're a married man,' he said to me.
'I know it,' I answered. 'Then what right did you
have to approach this girl?' 'I don't know,' I said,
'but I've been married twenty years and my wife is a
stringy woman with a bitter temper. And this girl
liked me and it was spring. And I said to myself:
here's this war and the world's gone cruel crazy and
pretty soon we'll all be dead and rotten. There was
a lilac bush in the garden and it was twilight and so
I kissed her a few times. And I almost thought I was
young again and back in the old country and life was
just beginning and there was peace and a little hope
and beauty in the world.' The boss looked at me as if
I was crazy. 'I'll have no immorality around here,'
he shouted. 'You're fired!' Now what sort of a man
is this? He called this immorality and I heard him
tell some young fellows about the immorality of going

to a street full of bawdy houses. He didn't pay any attention to things, you see. He just had a word— immorality—and it made him angry at others and satisfied with himself."

A word—and it made him angry at others and satisfied with himself. . . . Poor Benecke! He could get no more work in Central City. A Hun and probably, like all Huns, immoral to boot. He drifted away. But he had given me another definition of the evil malignity that lies at the root of moralistic generalizations and a fresh sense of what I knew to be the saving and triumphant virtue of the people to whom he belonged.

IV

Thus, too, to-day, poets and thinkers and publicists and millions of men and women are striving in Germany to re-understand and re-create a world in chaos. Once more in 1921 as in 1914 Germany leads the world in the production of books. There is trash enough— morbid rather than empty, as among us. But there are philosophies and visions so packed with thought and experience that the many thousands of people who buy and read them, as the editions show, must be admitted to possess a culture and a discipline of the mind and a knowledge of their own souls unheard of in any other age or land. Likewise the imaginative literature—novels and plays and especially the books of the new lyrical movement—is drawn from sources of perception and reflection which the average cultured reader in other countries has not yet reached within himself. I do not expect this thing which, for the sake of my own mind's integrity, I must assert, to be believed. Nothing is so deep-rooted in us as a sense of our ultimate superiority. We may appear to yield on this point or that. At the core of the self is a granite-hard conviction of the betterness of that self and its friends and its group. Such is the spiritual malady of the race. If once we could stop working with the concepts "better" and "worse" which we identify with higher and lower and so, in a primitive and subconscious way, with above and below in physical modes of being—master, slave, slayer, slain: if we could bring ourselves to think in terms of fruitful co-existent qualities in the psychical world, we would not struggle against such cognitions as I am trying to convey; we would have a much larger chance of deriving our self-respect from serenity and justice rather than from wilful ignorance and rage.

In Central City I once spoke to a colleague, a professor of political science, of the literature and art and thought of the Germans and of the wide dissemination of these things among the people and made a plea for an, at least, inquiring attitude toward such a nation. He replied that what I told him was doubtless true, but that it did not to his mind constitute a claim to high national culture which resided rather in political vigilance and political activity. I did not point out to him—he would have regarded it as presumptuous—the actual political supineness of Americans; their extreme suggestibility and their utter carelessness as to the quarters whence their winds of doctrine blow. I saw so clearly that he and I were shouting across a gulf. Literature and art and philosophy were to him not expressions and therefore forms of life, not the spiritual organs by which men understand and intercommunicate experience; they were to him decorative additions to life, like tin cornices on a shop front. And it would have been useless to tell him that the aesthetic and philosophical saturation of great masses of the German people had naturally led them to esteem political action lightly. For all such action implies hard limitation. To choose such action at all means a devotion to narrowly defined policies of whose insufficiency and mere opportunism the reflective mind is at once aware. Thus in every day life the unreflective man who is also the energetic one has the philosopher at his mercy. To know little is to dare easily, to have looked upon all sides of all mortal questions is to come near paralysis. Rude men in primitive communities pass judgment and execute sentences in matters that would have left Jesus dumb and Socrates puzzled. Then they ride off, these posses and lynchers, and eat their dinners in peace.

Yet the young poets in Germany who are listened to by thousands and thousands—Franz Werfel and Walter Hasenclever and many others—are crying out for more inwardness, not less, for a spiritualization and conquest and absorption into the mind of all things and all men; for a suspension of all moral judgment, all strife and for the remoulding of the world through love. They do not heed the traders and chafferers and diplomats—Stinnes no more than Morgan, Simons no more than Lloyd George. They are bent upon another business and men and women who lack bread and meat buy the books of these poets and creators of higher realities and go home and read and transcend hunger and cold, embargoes and reparations and the loss of mines. And they lift their heads from their books,

these readers, and hear that Lloyd George reaffirms
the single and absolute guilt of Germany in the war
and for a moment they remember a world which is still
ruled by such hollow and such savage fictions. But it
is only for a moment. Their bluish lids are lowered.
They read on. They are rebuilding the broken universe in their souls.

v

What could I do with this vision and this knowledge and this protest of mine in Central City? Men
talked such arrant nonsense that I committed a hundred indiscretions, overstated and misstated the intimate truths that I possessed and even, on the great
principle of John Stuart Mill that no truth, however
partial, needs so sorely to be emphasized as that which
a particular hour in history derides or disregards,
joined certain friends and colleagues in explaining to
a technically neutral country the political and military
actions of the German government. I did not count
the consequences nor, at bottom, greatly fear them.
Others were dependent on me and I did not dare to
fling away the meager sustenance which the university
doled out to me. But I knew very firmly, though I did
not always permit that knowledge to reach my consciousness, that life could not permanently be bounded
for me by that campus and that town. If by defending
my mind's integrity, a catastrophe came . . . well, I
almost awaited it as one awaits rain and thunder on
a day of unbearable sultriness.

When America entered the war the president of
the university sent for me. A tall, thick, old man with
a hoarse, monotonous voice and a large, determined,

self-righteous mouth. A mouth like William Jennings Bryan's—half business man's, half fanatic's. The intellectual equipment of a Presbyterian elder in a small town; the economic views of a professional strike-breaker tempered by a willingness to be charitable to the subservient poor; the aesthetic and philosophic vision of the Saturday Evening Post. He talked to me like a war editorial in the New York Evening Telegram and tried to make that talk persuasive to me. He who believed, let us say, in the virgin birth of Christ, tried to convince me that the countrymen of Dehmel and Hauptmann and Strauss and Einstein had mediaeval minds. A perverse imp leapt up in me. I translated some observations of Goethe and Shelley and John Stuart Mill and Whitman into his vernacular and spoke. His eyes grew a little hard and forbidding and shifted to the blotter on his desk. But he thought me more unpractical idealist—his euphemism for fool —than knave and promised, quite sincerely, that he would guard my interests unless his hand were forced. He made a virtue of this moral opportunism. Personally, he assured me, again sincerely, that he was willing to be tolerant; if the herd stampeded he would trample with the best. Such was the notion of democracy held by this essentially good and honest man.

I expected no more. But my friend, the professor of philosophy, failed me. Not personally. They were all kind enough. But intellectually. And that was worse. He who had always protested against the notion that truth could be discovered by committees now made the war-psychosis of the crowd his criterion of conduct and opinion. "How about the splendor of being in a minority, of resisting the mass, of suffering for an unpopular conviction?" I asked him. He stultified and denied himself, his intellectual past, his moral character. He thundered against the ninety-three German intellectuals who had believed what their government had told them and himself accepted as gospel the reports of the capitalistic and jingo press. The German intellectuals are dead or have recanted either explicitly in words or implicitly by supporting the revolution. My friend has not been heard from. He still teaches philosophy.

The crash came in a curious and, rightly looked upon, an amusing way. In 1916 I had published a little book on the modern movement in German literature. It was an unpolitical little book. It tried to convey a spirit, an atmosphere, a mood . . . to show that the best living writers were liberals, radicals, cultivators of a Goethean freedom. I said, among other things, that Nietzsche was indisputably one of the great masters of prose. The book fell into the hands of a real-estate broker. One must savor that fact. One must visualize the pudgy gentleman at his golden oak roll-top desk in his private office. He has been reading the editorial in his paper; he is fired to do his duty as a man and an American. There is something wonderful in the supreme innocence and directness of his mental processes. What, shall a man be supported by the people's money who glorifies that which our sons are going out to destroy at the cost of their blood? He summons his secretary who pats her sleek hair with brilliantly manicured fingers and shifts her chewing-gum to the other cheek. He dictates and a glow fills his bosom. The letter goes to the president and the deans of the university, to the governor of the state,

to the trustees, to senators. The real estate broker—
like Dwight Deacon in Zona Gale's excellent story—
goes virtuously home and, at the head of his domestic
board, impresses an admiring family with his patriotic
vigor, his acumen, his importance. He looks instruc-
tively over his glasses, then for a moment glumly:
"Vera, did I hear you giggle? You may leave the
table. Upon my word! Well, as I was saying: these
disloyalists . . . seditious talk . . . undermine morale
. . . contaminate the young . . . dooty of every wide
awake citizen. . . ." It goes on and on, the talk of
the eternal real estate broker, it goes on in peace as
well as in war: Be like me, be like me, think and feel
as I do, or I will drive you out, burn you, hang, draw
and quarter you and lick my lips at the trickle of your
blood. . . . And I, in my own small and dusty way,
was the eternal outcast, rebel, the other-thinking one—
guilty before the herd, guiltless in the dwelling-places
of the permanent, breaker of taboos, creator of new
values, doomed to defeat on this day in this little
grimy corner of the universe, invincible and inextin-
guishable as a type. Shall I ever conquer the real
estate broker? Shall I ever absorb him into myself?
And if I ever absorb him into myself shall I not be
he again? That is the question at the core of human
history. And it is fathomless.

VI

The president balked a little at the real estate
broker. Not for any deep reason. Only he had a dumb
feeling that the real estate broker was attacking the
thing from a wrong angle and interfering with his
own paternalistic and, upon the whole, humane and

kindly management of faculty affairs. Yet he was gradually being saved the nuisance of a final decision. The matter was being taken out of his hands.

The campus had been turned into a training-camp and swarmed with youths in khaki. They studied, slept, ate, drilled, talked in mechanically formed groups. A slow, stinging horror seized my flesh and crept into my bones. They were being trained to kill and be killed, to mutilate and to be mutilated. They were very cheerful. Each, at the innermost point of consciousness, carried the invincible, mystical assurance that he would come out unscathed. Each, like all of us, was unable to imagine his own death. For the universe is unimaginable to the individual without his consciousness of it: his perception of it creates and upholds it. Since he believes in its permanence, he believes, despite reason and experience, in his own. Such is the mystical and fatal delusion which, disguised under the names of patriotism, courage, sacrifice, makes conscription and modern war possible. If we could rip that delusion asunder, unswathe the consciousness of common men from these sticky layers, the enslaving state would crumble. The sight of those cheery, healthy boys turned me sick. I saw them blinded, waving bloody stumps, rotten with gangrene in trenches under fire. I rebelled against that place of irony and horror; I refused to take any precautions. A leprous sun seemed to burn over Central City. Middle-aged men and women roared and wheezed and sweated with hatred and patriotism and urged these young bodies to hasten to hurl themselves into blood and ooze and ordure.

An oily voice, a sleek, voluble voice with a hard

contradictory snicker in it came to me over the telephone. My presence was required on such a day at such an hour in the office of the district attorney. The voice purred reassuringly and then repeated the order with a sudden, lustfully cruel bark.

It was the owner of that voice who received me—white-haired, ruddy, cold-eyed but with a set, wheedling smile fixed under a thick, heavy, dogged nose. He took me into the district attorney's office, a large, square, ordinary lawyer's room with shabby desks and swivel chairs and rusty calf-skin volumes with red labels. Sharp sunshine poured in through the tall windows; a pigeon sped past; a bough tapped against the stonework. The district attorney sat back in his chair, a big, dark, bald man, not fat but fleshy; cold, meanly sensual, a careless begetter of children, a good "provider," a family man, a politician, a "handshaker." . . . He shook hands with me. I looked at his enormous cheeks, his small, official eyes. A huge expanse of shirt extended from his long chin to his belt. There was something monumental about the man, but also something obscene. I felt both the impenetrability of him and the raw, voracious appetites. He was, of all things, jovial! "Well, professor, I thought we'd better have a talk." His pretense that we were good fellows together was odious. "What have you against me?" I asked. He leaned forward. "A stack of evidence this high." "Let me see the evidence and confront me with the persons who provided it." "We don't do that," he snapped. "Then how can I tell what you're talking about?" He sat back comfortably and drawled: "Didn't you say that if America entered the war. . . ." I had, as a matter of fact, said none of the things he repeated. In the privacy of my office at the university I had made remarks that malice had twisted, broadened, coarsened and then communicated to him. I at once suspected the stupid woman who had probably written him anonymous letters. I pointed out to him that the evidence was garbled, not of a character that would be admitted in any American court of law and that it referred exclusively to the period of American neutrality during which, from the narrowest and most autocratic point of view, I had been free to say what I chose. Instead of replying he suddenly sprang up and roared. "What have you ever done to show your patriotism? What have you ever done for this country?" "I have taught and written. . . . ." He roared me down. "You liked to do that! What've you ever done for your country, I ask you!" The thing went on for an hour. I tried to reach his reason. He didn't want that to happen. At the end of the session he shook his head gloomily. He would see. . . .

Upon the whole he evidently thought me small game. Several influential members of the faculty wrote him in my behalf; the president sent him a message; he consented to my remaining in the service of the state. But I did not remain. The colleagues who pleaded for me did so not because they believed in freedom, but because they had a personal kindness for me and some respect for my character; the president protected me because he knew that I was poor and a good teacher and because he did not consider my wrongheadedness grave enough to warrant Mary's being exposed to material suffering. The tacit understanding was that I could buy a continued tenure of my job by silence, conformity, slavish submission. I asked for a sabbatical year that was due me and was granted the favor.

I fared very well and I am not insensitive to kindness. But what I had hoped for came from no quarter —a recognition, however faint, of the tenableness of my intellectual position. A German colleague, an exquisitely lovable, gifted, gentle soul, was fired without mercy. He was ill in body and had a frail wife—an American woman—and three small children. A poet and a philosopher, he wandered about selling books, tortured by the dull surfaces of an unfeeling world. He finally took a small position in Mexico. There, at the age of thirty-five, he died the other day. Hardship had undermined his strength; the process begun in Central City reached a fatal conclusion. Yet the men there knew the beauty of his mind, his complete political harmlessness, the fact that he had not come to us an immigrant but had been summoned as an exchange teacher to a great American University. But they were utterly callous to his fate. They had studied and philosophized with him and broken bread with him. They cast him out to die. . . .

Why did they relent to me? Because of the native tongue in my head, the things I had written, the fact that in all fundamental senses I am an American. A blind, half-conscious feeling of solidarity with me guided them, neither the idea of justice nor that of freedom. Yet this was a university and there they taught then and there they teach now Plato and Kant, Montaigne and Voltaire, Goethe and Shelley and even Walt Whitman who "beat the gong of revolt and stopped with them that plot and conspire."

[219]

CHAPTER X.

The World In Chaos

I

A quiet corner of old New York seemed a refuge from glare and hubbub. Around the corner was a tavern where one could drink beer and listen to music. The fiddlers were still Hungarians who played Grieg and even Brahms and Magyar dances and Russian folk-melodies. One could talk to one's friends in whatever language the mood and the subject demanded. We sat there even as other like-minded groups sat in London and Paris and Munich waiting for the madness of mankind to spend itself. The lamps of the tavern had orange-colored shades, the wainscoating was black with age. The place was filled with a soothing dusk and the blended odor of beer and tobacco and Wiener Schnitzel. I was, at least, back in civilization. There were no sweet slops; there was no gabble consisting largely of "dope," "guy," "sport," "case," "jazz," "Hun." It is quite easy to jest. But beneath the easy jest is a hard fact. Beer and wine and tobacco are the companions of poetry and philosophy and love; soda-water and banana-splits and sport not as a diversion but as a business, of moral lynching and the worst forms of sex slavery.

THE WORLD IN CHAOS

. . . That tavern is gone now, swept away by the barbarism of the Neo-Puritans.

For some weeks Mary and I relaxed our minds and nerves. But my resources would not permit me to remain quite idle and an old friend brought me the offer of a mastership in a private school. To teach English and Latin to boys seemed a tolerable enough prospect.

The huge building arises before me, the immense Y. M. C. A. building on the ninth floor of which the Harley School was housed. On the very first day of my activity a blast from some icy and infernal region seemed to smite my nerves. On the third day I knew that I had entered the lowest depth of civilization where there are elevators and modern plumbing and scientific ventilation and hygiene and cleanliness and morality and where the soul is dead. There were one hundred boys, varying in age from twelve to seventeen. They were nearly all the sons of wealthy tradesmen, brokers and manufacturers. They brought with them from their homes a stony contempt for literature, art and learning, for any form of reflection, for all tolerance, gentleness, humanity—for everything except money, machines and blind force when that force was exerted by them or in the direction of their strictly material interests. I did not make these observations hastily. I tried to exert a softening and a saving influence on one boy after another. So did one other member of the teaching staff—a cultivated, spiritual-minded, elderly New Englander. He and I compared notes day after day. We were dealing with souls killed by machines and by the doctrine of force before they had had a chance to be born. They listened to neither my old friend nor to me; they were impene-

trable to the simplest and most picturesque historical
or literary instruction. But they attended earnestly
to the malignant moral drivel of the Y. M. C. A. secretaries which consisted of two negative admonitions:
be ignorant of sex and drink no alcohol, and of one
positive one: smash!—smash the rival team, school,
and later the rival business or factory; smash the Hun
and the Bolshevik abroad; smash the other-thinking
one—liberal, socialist, foreigner—at home. And—this
was the constant corollary—in order to smash success-
fully, "get together," do team-work, never think, feel,
act, except with and through your particular pack.
This gospel of mass brutality and individual cowardice
and dishonor was studded in the chapel talks with the
names of successful men as exemplars—insurance
magnates, railroad kings, oil monopolists—and was
offered—such was the effrontery of these creatures—
in the name of Jesus of Nazareth.

The great steel and concrete building is in a shabby,
swarming neighborhood near a railroad station. There
are lunch rooms and open-air food-stands at every
corner. The waiting room of the railroad station is
always crowded. The pupils of the Harley school,
many of whom came to school in their motor cars,
were always talking about the "waps" and "dagos"
and "kikes" who drifted to and fro on those streets
and squares. They spoke of them and laughed with
a cold, empty derision, a curiously unmotivated malignity. How good those common people seemed to me;
how eloquent was the trouble and contemplation in
their eyes! I talked with the street-car men and ditch-
diggers, barbers and prostitutes. These people's natural thoughts were very far from the war. It had

been driven, an alien and meaningless thing, into their consciousness. "The kings made it," they said, "the rich made it." An unlettered Lithuanian plasterer said: "Life is hard in Central Europe. The people have not land enough to grow their own food. Either the big rulers, East and West, must parcel out the world-markets justly or there will be famine and revolution." He caught sight of a policeman and added as by rote: "I'm for the allies. Too much militarism in Germany."

There was a school supper and I met the fathers of my pupils. They were mellower, of course, and their manners and speech were suaver. But they made the psychical picture complete. Their contempt for any form of thinking was indescribable. In their minds the universe was like the blue-print of a machine. Every detail was fixed and provided for and established by some sanction which they could not explain but would not endure to have questioned. I deliberately conversed in terms that differed slightly, but only slightly, from the verbal formulae of the conventional newspaper and the Y. M. C. A. secretaries concerning the world situation. Fourteen hours later a rumor had reached the head-master that there was an unsafe man in his school.

A good many intellectuals, deceived by historical analogies, by the public gifts of a few super-plutocrats, by a fitful patronage of the arts exercised by wealthy Jews, assign to the financial and industrial bosses the qualities and functions of an oligarchy. But the oligarchs are rich without splendor and powerful without imagination. They are not Medici; they are not even Junkers. They are only grocers. These men of

large affairs have pigmy intelligences, the moral prejudices of villagers, the tastes not even of the tap-room,
but of the "parlor." They influence legislation and
own the press and we have prohibition, censorships,
vice crusades. They are not aristocrats on the lowest
plane. They are not even amusing like the Prince
Regent and his strutting "bucks," not even picturesque and cynical like the French gentlemen of the
ancien régime; they are stupid, uninteresting, meanly
barbarous.

II

The posters on the walls and fences bothered me.
Do you remember them? "The Prussian Cur," "The
Hun, His mark." These posters with their splashes
of crude red and their pictures of ape or wolf-like
creatures bore no relation, of course, either to the
people against whom they were directed nor to the
minds of the combatants on either side. They revealed
a brutality and obscenity in the spirits that conceived
and the hands that executed them which kindled in
me a little flame of terror at the civilization which,
unconsciously but firmly, I had always held to be fun-
damentally humane and secure. Nothing seemed impossible any longer. The barbarities of history, the
sacking of cities, the useless slaughter of men, the selling of people into slavery, the butchery for matters
of opinion and conscience—all these had been but as
pictures of perished things to heighten by a melancholy yet not unpleasing contrast the glow of one's
own hearth, the serenity of one's mind. All that faith
in the sure, essential decency of life was broken. No
wonder that the courts passed inhuman sentences, that

men were mobbed and lynched and tortured in prisons and that the newspapers grew daily more lecherous in their appetite for blood. . . .

The songs in the music-halls bothered me.

> "America, she needs you like a mother.
> Will you throw your mother down? . . .

> "Like Washington crossed the Delaware
> Pershing will cross the Rhine."

The crafty blending here of natural pieties with pack-ferocity and pack-pride was hit upon by an old and deadly instinct. Love was played upon and lurking fear. To stamp out from the beginning any stirring of humane compunction, the public enemy was carefully stripped of any of the characteristics that distinguish man. Another very old and very effective trick. "You are not dealing, countrymen," Cicero said in his fourth invective against Antony, "you are not contending with an enemy with whom any sort of peace is possible. For he does not merely, as he once did, desire your slavery, but in his madness lusts for your very blood. His favorite game is one of blood, of slaughter, of murdering citizens openly. You are not dealing, fellow citizens, with a criminal and wicked man, but with a monstrous and loathesome beast. . . . cum immane tætraque belua. . . . " (I tried to point out the analogy to my pupils. They nudged each other. They were sure I was quite mad.)

I used to watch the great audiences in the music-halls. There were no mobile faces, no speaking faces, nor many such as showed the scars of passionate excitement or searching experience. Neither were there spiritualized and contemplative faces. The passions behind these eyes were not spent, nor were they subdued; they were neither exercised nor controlled. They were hounds not held in leash by their owners, but leashless hounds that cringed and fawned before the visible lash and rod of this society and morality with its peculiar law and order. Native or foreign born, Jew or Gentile—these faces were the faces of modern Christians: natural, pagan men living under the legalized tyranny of the sickly asceticism of Paul. Fear aping solemn resignation, or flabby, elderly content was in their eyes and on the countenances of the young a furtive gaiety, a harsh, empty delight conscious of its own brevity and unimportance in a world given over to morality and business. . . . No inner pride, no natural erectness sustained these souls. So, in their drained and inhibited lives, they fasten their pride to mean things—skill at a foolish game, a garment, a bit of cooking, a personal oddity, a tawdry virtue lacked by a neighbor. But these things do not suffice. There is always to be observed a background of querulous irritation. Hence, by a pitiful device, men transfer their pride to forces outside of themselves—a fraternal order, their bosses, the state. When the poor muddle-headed, enslaved clerk says: "My concern did a three million dollar business last year," or "America can lick creation," he substitutes an alien and essentially hostile force for his own soul which that very force has robbed of the power of being self-sustaining, happy and free. Therefore when, during the last year of the war, I heard these audiences bay and cheer the foul attacks upon an enemy who was not theirs, since there is no such thing as enemy except in an evil and constructive and lying sense, and when I saw them transfer their self-respect to their slave-driver, the moral and political state, I had an old, old vision—the huge, monstrous idol, the sacrificial fires, the victims driven by a lust for self-immolation into the scorching flames. Yes, those dim, far-off ancestors of mine had laid hold upon a profound truth: idols are purely evil. Alas, they themselves set up the most menacing of idols—a theocratic state. And that state persists. For the modern state, whenever it is most hotly bent upon oppression within and slaughter without, declares that good and therefore God are on its side, that it, indeed, embodies the purposes of God, and so the state becomes theocratic by its own fiat and an idol and men, who are worshipping animals, writhe in their blood and shame and spiritual nakedness at the idol's feet.

A black year. The war-fever throbbed. The boys at the Harley school turned to me each day their burnished and impenetrable faces. My father died. A subtly but relentlessly hostile environment and an unworthy occupation had long ago broken him. His mind had slipped into a twilight region of settled despair. In one of his last moments of lucidity he had spoken sorrowfully of the war and hummed an air of Mozart and then wept gently. Thereafter he sank into an unrelieved melancholy. When he came to die there was nothing more to be hoped for him and so I felt no pang for his death, only for his life and into my mind there streamed once more the strange and to me so strangely freighted sunshine of Queenshaven. I sat beside his body, pondering upon his fate, resolved to speak for him a word that he himself had had no power to utter.

UP STREAM

All things hurt him. He struck out
To help him in the unequal bout;
Knowing he was doomed to lose
He hid with laughter cut and bruise
And jeered in desperate wildness since
He dared not let men see him wince.
In his worst stridency he knew
That some said "vulgar," some said "Jew,"
And held in frantic leash a whole
World's sorrow in his stricken soul.

Yet he was patient, brave and kind
While stood the stronghold of his mind,
And coming from the shop or street
Where he had chaffered in the heat,
He built a world beyond the dim
Visions of them who wounded him.
Secure from them he ceased to scoff,
Stripped the ignoble gesture off,
Frugal in every common want
He played Beethoven and read Kant.

Now on his forehead blends with love
The dignity life robbed him of,
And on his dead and shrunken face
Falls the grandeur of his race.

III

Armistice day came with its sharp though barren
relief at the ending of the mere butchery. The Germans had laid down their arms. Wilson's fourteen
points were to reshape the world. Then came the
Judas trick of Versailles, the tricking not only of Germany but, as is already abundantly clear, of all mankind. "If you would know what a war was about,"
H. A. Brailsford memorably said, "study the terms of

peace." The great capitalistic groups who control industrial populations had come to blows over coal and oil and tropical estates and trade-routes. The Western group won and proceeded to ruin its chief competitor. If millions of innocent people, including their own, if all the true goods of civilization, if sanity and honor went down to disaster in the process—what did it matter to them? They are still busy reducing Europe to chaos and they are still talking in terms of guilt and moral idealism. If they were honestly brutal the ruin might be mitigated. There is something respectable and wholesome about a Fisher or a Tirpitz. The lion can be caged or shot and still considered a not ignoble brute. Let him begin to rip out the bowels of men and crunch the bones of little children in the name of this man's good and that man's moral castigation, and he becomes immeasurably more formidable as well as profoundly loathsome.

The cynical observer, were one not too depressed to be cynical, could enjoy, as never before, the spectacle of the confused antics of mankind. Auckland Geddes, the British ambassador, blurts out a partial but very important truth: "Germany was being forced into a position with rising food costs—look at the change in the price of wheat in the first ten years of this century —Germany was being forced into a position in which she almost had to fight." But Makino, the Japanese ambassador, ignorant, if one will believe it, of the "pacification" of Korea and the theft of huge Asian territories, declares: "Absolute and sincere repentance—published repentance—without reserve and without any attempt to save Germany's face is the cornerstone upon which must rest any restoration of confidence." Repentance for what—the rising price of food? Or the growth of population? No, the sturdy democratic citizen answers, for William II! That is the cynic's triumphant moment. For he does indeed see an element of guilt in a great modern people's permitting itself to be swayed by an orthodox Christian, an amateur moralist, a romantic jingo, a mystical nationalist. But the average conservative American—pillar of a church, supporter of the anti-saloon league, member of defense committees and fraternal orders, proclaimer of America's moral mission—what right has he to protest against William II? He *is* William II. He glories in the rule of weak-minded assent to dogma, rancid romanticism, far-flung navies, glittering armaments. He lets the Congress spend the greater part of the nation's income on what is called national defense and means international provocation. The religion of his fathers and loyalty to his country, right or wrong, are good enough for him. So, precisely, were they for William II. It is quite true that stupidity rules. It rules the world.

IV

I was enabled to leave the Harley school and take up an occupation for which I am reasonably well fitted and which I found more satisfying to the mind than any in which I had yet engaged. Quieter moods came to me, though often still for months I saw in nightmare or in sudden, waking vision those spick and span classrooms, those keen, metallic faces and heard the cackle and clatter of those insufferably alien voices. I found, too, that the long noise and agitation of the war had paralysed the power of seeing, of absorption, that it had estranged me from beautiful and enduring things.

An autumn came which was like a return home. Once more I saw shadows on the river and bronze foliage and laid my palms against the cool trunks of trees. Once more with less of inner fever to disturb my sight I was able to survey the American scene.

The end of the war left us, as it left other parts of the world, in an uproar of reaction and nationalism—the two delusions that repression destroys and that uniformity is admirable. The fact that history flatly contradicts the first of these assumptions and the whole course of nature the latter seems to trouble no one. We have something very like witch-hunts upon any one, especially in the public service, who is suspected of having seriously reflected upon political or economic questions; we have a nation-wide, organized effort to break down the slow gains of labor; we have a revival of the Ku Klux Klan, outbreaks of smouldering race animosities and the apparently inevitable recrudescense of Jew baiting. The nation demands, as the cant of the day has it, one hundred per cent Americanism.

It is time for some one to speak a little boldly and a little rudely concerning these childish fallacies. Wherever two or three Americans of German descent gather they talk about their loyalty to the constitution and humbly submit that they ask nothing but the minimum rights guaranteed to obedient citizens of the sovereign and omnipotent state; wherever two or three Americans of Jewish descent gather they explain to each other, for the benefit of the public (including

Henry Ford) that only one—or is it two?—of the chief commissars of the Federated Socialist Soviet Republic is Jewish and that so and so many Jewish boys fought to make the world safe for one group of predatory imperialisms at the expense of another group. The Irish alone, by virtue of something proud and fiery and reckless in their nature, seem reasonably free from this foolish and futile form of spiritual subservience.

The good man who is also the good citizen is the man of self-governed mind and self-originating vision. "I think a man's first duty," said Mark Twain, "is to his honor, not to his country and not to his party." And by honor he meant the honor of the mind. Establish your convictions on as sound a basis as you can; then cling to them. That is the only loyalty that has any value. The mob that demands conformity of you has no claim on your obedience. "It is made up of sheep;" to quote Mark Twain once more, "it is governed by minorities, seldom or never by majorities. It suppresses its feelings and beliefs and follows the handful that makes the most noise." To yield to public clamor is, therefore, not only to betray yourself but to give up the duty—your single duty—of creative activity within the social group in which you live. Unscrupulous journalists, dependent on narrow capitalistic interests, may whip up public passion against you. As for the public itself? "The idea of what the public will think," Hazlitt wrote with that triumphant sagacity of his, "prevents the public from ever thinking at all, and acts as a spell on the exercise of private judgment, so that in short the public ear is at the mercy of the first impudent pretender who chooses to fill it with noisy assertions, or false surmises or secret whispers. What is said by one is heard by all; the supposition that a thing is known to all the world makes all the world believe it, and the hollow repetition of a vague report drowns the still, small voice of reason." Thus comes about the intimidation through the mob which has no kinship with any service of the people. It must always be remembered that "self-government" is not, alas, as John Stuart Mill justly pointed out, "the government of each by himself, but of each by all the rest. The people consequently may desire to oppress a part of their number; and precautions are as much needed against this as against any other abuse of power." On the subject of liberty there can be no compromise. You compromise liberty and betray the Republic when you practise unwilling conformity or offer a propitiatory obedience to foreheads of brass and lungs of leather. For liberty, in the great words of Lord Acton, "means the assurance that every man shall be protected in doing what he believes to be his duty against the influence of authority or majorities, opinion or custom."

The practice of such liberty does not, as you will be told, diminish a nation's power, only its truculence and pugnacity. Nor should it be suspended but all the more scrupulously exercised in times of war or the danger of war when passion drowns all remnants of reflection, terror begets hatred and hatred slavery and destruction. The cry of defense is a trick. No numerous and powerful people, at any rate, wages an unavoidable and purely defensive war. Nor is victory a necessity or even necessarily a blessing. It is already apparent that the best and truest friends of the French

Republic were the "defeatists" of 1916 and 1917. There is no certain good but truth, no certain effectiveness but in an abstention from all force, no final consolation save the integrity of one's own mind.

V

The question of the nature of loyalty and liberty is, once closely thought upon, plain enough. More intricate, at least in appearance, is the problem of nativism and the enforcement of cultural solidarity on the assumption that this country harbors hosts and guests. The assumption, being built upon an absurd analogy, is baseless. The earth belongs to mankind and all early history is the history of migrations. No people in the world is dwelling in the land of its origin. The Greeks came from we know not where and occupied the penninsula and the islands that are their historic home; tribes from the North West of Germany sailed to Britain and made it England. The discovery of America caused a late and perhaps last migratory movement in which, so long as land and air are here and over-population or war or persecution elsewhere, all mankind has the biological and moral right to participate. Priority of settlement gives no right to the exercise of exclusion. Moreover the life of nations is, humanly speaking, of enormous duration. In the perspective of historic time the intervals that separate the coming of the early English and Dutch from that of the early German or even Jewish settlers will shrink to absurdly inconsiderable proportions. Whoever is here, whoever comes here, has a right to be here and, since he submits to laws, a right to his share in destroying or in making them.

That a nation possessing a compact and autonomous culture should desire recent additions to its population to merge into its cultural life and enrich that life is natural. But the process must come from within. So soon as outer urgency is applied the inner necessity and, therefore, the spiritual justification of the process itself stands in grave doubt. No Anglicization committees produced Dante Gabriel Rossetti or Joseph Conrad, no Germanization committees produced Adelbert von Chamisso or Hugo von Hofmannsthal, no movement for the assimilation of foreigners made French poets of Francis Vielé-Griffin or Stuart Merrill. Beautiful things are beloved because they are beautiful, because there is in them an irresistible attractiveness, because they are conformable to the needs of the soul. The very existence of an Americanization movement shows—when every allowance for our peculiar conditions has been made—a discord, a prematureness; it shows a crudeness in the fruits of our civilization which not force and clamor but only time and the sun can ripen.

Americanization means, of course, assimilation. But that is an empty concept, a mere cry of rage or tyranny, until the question is answered which would never be asked were the answer ripe: Assimilation to what? To what homogeneous culture, to what folkways of festival and song, to what common instincts concerning love and beauty, to what imaginative passions, to what roads of thought? We have none such that can unite us. Two things are nation wide and engage the passions of the Anglo-American stock: baseball and the prohibition of wine, love, speculation and art. Is the sharing of these two passions to mark the assimilated American? I shall be accused of a perverse injustice. Quite wrongly. For the notion of liberty on which the Republic was founded, the spirit of America that animated Emerson and Whitman, is vividly alive to-day only in the unassimilated foreigner, in that pathetic pilgrim to a forgotten shrine. The prohibitionists of Kansas, the lynchers of Georgia, the hard-headed businessmen in the chambers of commerce in a thousand cities, the members of the National Security League, The American Legion, The Loyal American League—what have these self-appointed inquisitors and Black Hundreds to do with liberty? "Every man and woman who will not get in line must get out!" Such is the avowed program of the Loyal American Legion. Such has been the program of every instigator of massacre or pogrom in history. These people suspect liberty, just as they suspect civilized food and drink, art, personal relations, as symptoms of an alien and subversive spirit.

One cultural tradition we have in America and it is, by at least a few years, the oldest: the linguistic and literary tradition of the English race. But that tradition—the tradition of Chaucer and Shakespeare and Milton——is a learned and aristocratic one. It has never humanized the folk of the British motherland. How many Anglo-Americans share it? Ask the members of the local chapter of the American Legion when, in the name of American culture, they annoy a German Singing Society—ask them to quote fifty lines from the fundamental classics of the English tongue! How many immigrants, then, can share that tradition or become assimilated to it? One, perhaps one, in every million. I am that one in a million. What Anglo-American has lived with the poets who are the sources of his great tradition more closely than I? What Anglo-American has a deeper sense for the order and eloquence and beauty of his own tongue than I? But when, in old days, I desired to translate my Americanism in that high and fine sense into action, I was told that I was not wanted. Yet I was to be Americanized. I am even now to be assimilated. Suppose I intend rather to assimilate America, to mitigate Puritan barbarism by the influence of my spirit and the example of my life? Then a writer named, let us say, Stuart Sherman, declares that I pervert the national genius. But suppose I am the national genius—Dreiser and Mencken and Francis Hackett and I—rather than Stuart Sherman or the late Hamilton Wright Mabie or the smoothly assimilated Edward Bok? Ah, if we could but all meet in the year two-thousand before some great and spiritual tribunal. Until some such day comes the question must remain an open one. . . .

The common folk cannot make my original choice nor suffer my exclusion. An old and perhaps wearisome story is to be told of them, but a story that must be told again and again until a sense of true liberty and of human values breaks in upon the darkness and the degradation of our day.

I knew an old Jew from the South of Russia. He wore a long beard and you could see where his ear-locks had been. He had a habit of hiding his hands in his sleeves. He read the Torah and the legends of his people in the sacred tongue. He read Hamlet and Faust in Yiddish translations. He read not only the

political news but also the well-conducted literary
columns in the Yiddish papers and cast a thoughtful
vote. He sat in his café on Second Avenue and discussed many notable matters and drank tea and, occasionally, a thimble-full of brandy and smoked Russian cigarettes. He was a wise man and a charitable
one and died poor. His son has become Americanized.
He knows neither Hebrew nor Yiddish. His English
is less foreign than his father's was, but far more
vulgar and corrupt. On his clean-shaven face there
is an indescribable blending of impudence and cun-
ning, servility and smartness. He is manager of the
Lake City Emporium, makes big money and thinks
the old man was a little weak in the head. He says,
having just made another particularly unscrupulous
five-thousand: "Yes sir, I'm an American all right.
This country is good enough for me." He likes to see
a game of baseball and sometimes drowses over the
Saturday Evening Post. His fat, sleek, indolent,
young wife blazes with diamonds. . . .

I knew an old German grocer from Mecklenburg.
He loved the poems of Claus Groth, the Low German
Burns, and quoted largely and with a fine, ripe appre-
ciation from the books of Fritz Reuter. He read Low
German papers. He was a member of a singing society and was unlearned neither in the great folk-songs
of his people nor in the works of Schubert and Schumann. He quenched his moderate thirst with beer.
His English was broken to the last. But in the American community which was his home for forty years
his name stood for careful honor and frugal wisdom.
His son has become Americanized. He reads the colored Sunday supplements of the yellow press. He is

a baseball "fan;" his favorite songwriter is Irving Berlin; he drinks whiskey—on the sly. He wants a political job in order "to live on easy street." Meanwhile he clerks around. Having exchanged his father's game of skat for poker he ran through his inheritance in two years in gambling rooms. He has Anglicized his name. . . .

These are unhappily not extreme cases. They are not rare. They are increasing in frequency under the pressure of tribal tyranny. Nor have they, as I shall be glibly and vaguely told, anything to do with character. For the basic truth of the matter lies here: If you drain a man of spiritual and intellectual content, if you cut him off from the cultural continuity that is native to him and then fling him into a world where his choice lies between an impossible religiosity and Prohibition on the one hand, and the naked vulgarity of the streets and of the baseball diamond on the other, you have robbed him of the foundation on which character can be built. The slow gains of the ages are obliterated in him. He uses the mechanics of civilization to become a sharper or a wastrel.

Mr. Granville Barker, the British playwright, tells a story which he will forgive me for borrowing. He was taking a walk in spring on Staten Island. It was Sunday. Behind a hedge sat an Italian laborer with all the grime of the week on him, munching dark bread and garlic and reading with great intensity. Mr. Barker caught a glimpse of the book. It was a cheap, well thumbed edition of the Divine Comedy. "The children of this man," said Mr. Barker, "will probably be Americanized. They will be cleaner and have better wages and eat daintier food and perhaps have electric light in their houses. But will they sit behind a hedge on Sunday reading an American Divine Comedy of the future?"

The doctrine of assimilation, if driven home by public pressure and official mandate, will create a race of unconscious spiritual helots. We shall become utterly barbarous and desolate. The friend of the Republic, the lover of those values which alone make life endurable, must bid the German and the Jew, the Latin and the Slav preserve his cultural tradition and beware of the encroachments of Neo-Puritan barbarism —beware of becoming merely another dweller on an endless Main Street; he must plead with him to remain spiritually himself until he melts naturally and gradually into a richer life, a broader liberty, a more radiant artistic and intellectual culture than his own.

VI

I gravely fear that he will not be permitted to heed the warning. Those who have the whip will not lay it aside. For the evils that are done and suffered in human society flow from one source and that source is hardest to reach. Probe to the core of any man's consciousness and you will come upon a blind and stony kernel of moral certitude. He has taken his accidental tastes, beliefs, instincts, and has transformed them into an absolute. Church, synagogue and mosque tell him that this complex of instincts and opinions forged into solidity by his will to conquer is the command of God. The so-called liberal who rejects a revelation still harbors the unbreakable conviction that his moral faith is supported by a super-personal sanction and wreaks his set of habits upon his fellows in the name of some concept to which he assigns a false universality. Thus the religious man, the righteous man, the patriot, each is convinced that he knows what is absolutely right and hence is justified in enforcing his rightness and its practices upon those whom he considers weak, wrong-headed and perverse. From the entertaining of such moral absolutes to the lynching stake and the torture chamber the path, both logical and practical, is straight and unreturning. The man who believes that his moral rightness is absolute, though he himself never touches the hair of another's head, is a murderer and the accomplice of murderers. For only from moral certitude can arise the exertion of force over others. To avert your face from a neighbor who believes that society needs a different distribution of property or that love is a personal and not a legal matter is to lay hands of violence upon his soul. To wage war for an island or a coal-field is evil enough. But to wage it with an assurance of one's moral rightness and the enemy's moral wrongness reduces men, as we of this generation have witnessed, below the fiercest and dullest beasts. To fight for the right is the last of human follies and degradations. It is to identify yourself with God in order to be cruel without the temptation of a humane relenting. By the delusion of absolute moral knowledge and by no other means can the patient and kindly children of the earth be turned into brutes with nerves of wire and hearts of granite. When the great revolution broke out in Russia I felt a glow and a brief hope. But that glow and that hope are also fading. For the purpose of an economic revolution is to release man from physical suffering and uncertainty and the resultant slavery in order that the individual may be set wholly free; it is not to cage and herd him into another exclusive ideology with its dogmas, laws and prophets. The aim of ultimate revolution must be to destroy the herd and the herd mind and the herd mind's hardening into that moral faith from which are born persecution and disease and war.

So at the end of this journey of the mind I reach the goal of ancient but eternal platitudes. No change will avail in this world except an inner change. There is no absolute but life, but the persistence of the individual and so of the race. No God has spoken, no sanction exists. There is no inherent reason why men should own property privately or in common, why they should practice monogamy or some other form of sexual union. Their aim being happiness and their happiness consisting in beautiful and rational living, it must be their purpose to discover what actions and agreements will lead to such living. The conservative replies that these actions and agreements have been discovered. The free man's terrible and sufficient answer must be a picture of the world at the end of twenty centuries of capitalism and Christian morals. It is a strange fallacy to regard unanimity as desirable. Were men unanimous they would be animals with the monotonous instincts of animals and the forever changeless and recurrent gestures of those instincts. Varieties of spiritual temper and outer experience make life human. Each variety has relative truth, relative value, relative beauty for him who is impelled to live it. So soon as he seeks to impose its dictates upon another, he asserts its absoluteness and not only commits a crime but destroys the multiplicity that makes the cosmos and invites the featureless monotony that is the negation of it. He may persuade others by being or pleading, never by acting. To deflect is to wound and even to touch is to kill. And life, life only, not one kind of life rather than another, is sacred. This sacredness must be felt by the soul. We must learn to shrink from any exertion of force as we do normally from murder. We must give up emotionally the moral legends that justify our tyrannies. The words of Shelley must be accepted literally. Man is to be "free, uncircumscribed," he is to be

> Exempt from awe, worship, degree, the king
> Over himself;

he is to liberate himself from "guilt and pain"

> Which were for his will made or suffered then.

Severely practical consequences arise from such a conception of human existence. During the fiscal year of 1920 ninety-two per cent of the national expenditure of this country went for the army, the navy and the results of war. The present fiscal year promises to repeat the story. Thus over four billions of dollars will be spent on the consequences and preparations of destruction. These are figures to make the imagination halt. But analyze them and conceive of this vast wealth spent annually, even within the present economic order, on unemployment and old age insurance, education and the endowment of motherhood. At once the picture of life undergoes a radical change. There are minor but still considerable sources of waste. Millions are spent on missionary work—the feeble impudence of teaching other races a set of legends and a bankrupt system of conduct; other millions are spent on vice crusades, on the persecution of prostitutes and on the enforcement of unpopular, repressive laws. The children of New York city have not school houses enough for the most elementary instruction and the courts are asking the inhabitants of the city to raise twenty-seven millions of dollars to defray the cost of prosecuting infringements of the eighteenth amendment. It may be doubted whether deliberate human folly has gone beyond that in any age or among any people apparently civilized. Let us suppose the funds of the missionaries and the vice crusaders spent for the medical research of venereal diseases. In one generation the physiology and psychology of human love would be revolutionized and saved. This, together with the elimination of the savage notion of illegitimacy, the endowment of voluntary motherhood, the universal introduction of efficient contraceptives, would transform millions of lives that are now stagnant and foul morasses into free rivers flowing in the sun. Why do we waste the wealth produced by human labor on crippling our own instincts and hounding our own souls? Why do we, pitiful slaves, toil to make the knout that flays our living flesh? Because we let stupid zealots persuade us that their sadism is a moral absolute compulsive on our minds and actions. And because men are starved in all their vital impulses and robbed of all delight and liberty they sigh for immortality as the forlornest of mortal hopes, for a Mohammedan heaven of sensuous compensation, which is the more honest one, or a Christian heaven in which all that is human will be extinguished and trouble them no more. The philosopher, driven by a noble urge, seeks to make rational his universe by assigning to creative values a permanent validity. I share that speculative hope. But I deplore its exploitation by moralistic professors who play into the hands of them that stunt and defile the life of man. . . . I see old men with vague, wandering eyes and thin, drawn lips and claw-like fumbling hands. They mutter in the churches; they confer with priests; they make gifts to buy their way to heaven past old thefts and stealthy lecheries. Morality has disinherited and poisoned them. They want another chance; they want to be cleansed. . . . I have a vision of an old man of a new moral order. Neither you nor I will be that man. But the hope of his coming may sustain us He, too, has been touched by fleshly decay. But his wrinkles do not humiliate him; his white hair does not tell him that it is too late. His eyes are serene and full of memories. He has worked at his chosen task without fear of penury; he has loved freely and magnificently. . . . The voice of one—what a trick of laughing at the dawn she had—floats to him . . . the sombre brows and hair of another—what splendor was hers of mind and passion—arise before him. . . . Yes, beauty is immortal and of immortal goodness. . . . He thinks of evenings in gardens by a river where over wine, amber or the color of dark rose-leaves, he and his friends debated of art and the state and the procession of history and the nature of the unfathomable world. He thinks of his strong children living in the sun. He sits in an armchair by the window, a volume of Plato or Goethe on his knees. The sun is setting for him now. But he is beyond wanting, needing, striving. He has had his dawn, his noon, his afternoon. The sun sinks and darkness falls upon the open page. If there is life beyond earth he is unafraid. If there is none, he is at peace. Work, loveliness and wisdom have been his. The end is as fit as the beginning; the darkness is as beautiful as the dawn.

EPILOGUE

All that I have written is true. It is true of America. It is true, in other degrees, of mankind. But I have written of America for the simple reason that I am an American and I have spoken strongly for the equally simple reason that the measure of one's love and need is also the measure of one's disappointment and indignation.

The facts stand as I have recorded them. And the implications stand. Among the masses of our countrymen I see no stirring, no desire to penetrate beyond fixed names to living things, no awakening from the spectral delusions amid which they pursue their aimless business and their sapless pleasures. But the critical spirit which is also the creative spirit has arisen among us and it has arisen, naturally and inevitably, in the form of a protest and a rebellion against the life and the ethos which is also described here. I need but name a few representative names: Masters, Sherwood Anderson, Sinclair Lewis. The substance of our new literature, of poems and novels and books of criticism, is clearly this: Life among us is ugly and mean and, above all things, false in its assumptions and measures. Somehow we must break these shackles and flee and emerge into some beyond of sanity, of a closer contact with reality, of nature and of truth.

A few of the books of our new writers are read by

many for the story, as a matter of fashion, often quite unreflectively. But most of them are read by a handful of people only. This handful means little among our overwhelming numbers and we who love this new literature and are sustained by it are often deceived in regard to its significance as either a symptom or a sanative. Shall I now say, in order to end agreeably: It is always darkest before dawn? No; for that kind of professional optimism is precisely one of our national vices. The hour is dark. But that shall not prevent us from working and striving for a better one that may come hereafter.

THE END